The Best of
THAI
CUISINE

Sisamon Kongpan

D0474643

แสงแดด

Sangdad Books

National Library of Thailand Cataloging in Publication Data

The Best of Thai Cuisine.--Bangkok : Sangdad, 1999.

176 p.

1. Cookery, Thai. I. Title.

641.5

ISBN 974-7163-99-3

Sangdad Books
Published by Sangdad Publishing Co.,Ltd.
320 Lat Phrao 94 (Town in Town)
Wongthonglang, Bangkok 10310, Thailand
Tel. (662) 538-7576, 538-5553, 934-4411
Fax : (662) 538-1499
e-mail : sangdad@asianet.co.th

Director: Nidda Hongwiwat
Editor: Nidda Hongwiwat
Editor's Assistant: Obchery Imsabai
Photography: Sangdad Studio
Design: Samart Sudto
Lay Out: Rungrudee Panichsri
Illustration: Sarayut Yoosuk
Marketing Director: Waynisa Chotiaroon
Production Director: Jiranun Tubniem

CONTENTS

ONE-PLATE DISHES

SWEETS

FRUIT JUICES

INTRODUCTION

That you have gotten so far into this book as to begin reading the introduction likely indicates that you are no stranger to Thai food and that you have a more-than-casual interest in doing some real Thai cooking. If so, read on, for this book presents recipes for a generous selection of dishes as they are prepared by and for Thais themselves. In particular, the recipes represent the cuisine of Bangkok, probably the most varied in the country.

The recipes have been developed and refined by a leading expert on thai cookery, Sisamon Kongphan, a home economist educated in Thailand and the United State, who currently teaches at the Department of Home Economics of the Institute of Technology and Vocational Education in Bangkok, a post she has held since 1974. Sisamon has spent a considerable part of her career in her cookery laboratory, where one of her major concerns has been systematizingt the "pinch-of-this-dash-of-that" sort of measurement so typical of traditional Thai cookery. In her more than three decades as a teacher, Sisamon has had thousands of students, some from far away as Japan and America, and she has reached many more through her video tape and her publications. She is the author of more than ten cookbooks on Thai as well as other cuisine and contributes regulary to the cooking pages of leading magazines and newspapers. Her recipes are thus accurate and thoroughly tested.

Here at the outset it is well to say something about certain procedures used in preparation of the dishes. The object of much Thai cookery is to produce something to be eaten with rice. It is rice, all, that for thousands of years has supported the peoples of the river valleys that today comprise Thailand. Rice provides the wherewithal for life; other foods make eating rice more enjoyable and interesting. Now, to be eaten with rice, a food should, first, be in a form such that it can be mixed with rice easily, and secondly, be extremely flavorful so as to be tasty after being diluted by mixing with rice. Consequently, to facilitate mixing and to release their full flavor, many ingredients are cut into small pieces or pounded to paste.

For cutting, an assortment of knives and a sturdy chopping block, often a section of the trunk of a tamarind tree, are standard, equipment. It is with a knife and the block that chopped meats are made; although if you wish, you may use a meat grinder or purchase ground meats at the butcher's. Also note that in some of the recipes in this book, the quantities of such ingredients as the gingers, lemon grass, and coriander root are given in spoonsful, and so these must be sliced up into small pieces in order to be measured.

Pounding is done with mortar and pestle. Inexpensive but serviceable glazed earthenware mortars are used with hardwood pestles. More lasting is a mortar and pestle of stone, for the stone remains smooth and easy to clean. A disadvantage of stone is the weight, and so it is wise to consider carefully your actual needs, and then to buy the smallest stone mortar that will meet them. When available, an electric blender can undertake much of the work of the mortar and pestle.

Prior to pounding, some ingredients are roasted to soften them, to dry them so they crumble more easily, or to release flavor and aroma. Roasting is typically done over a bed of coals. Large items can be placed on a gridiron over the coals. Smaller items such as shallots or chillies are impaled on bamboo skewers and then placed on the gridiron. Seeds, such as coriander and cumin seeds and also peanuts, are parched, or pan roasted: they are placed in a dry frying pan (kra-tha) over low heat and continually stirred with a spatula until done. In all roasting, a low heat and regular turning are necessary to ensure that the items are evenly heated throughout. When available, an oven can be used for roasting.

Once ingredients are prepared, they are often combined in a frying pan. The frying pan (kra-tha, กระทะ) has a round, rather than a flat, bottom. Because of the curvature, most of the oil collects in a pool, so relatively little oil need be put in the pan to obtain a good depth of hot oil to fry spices, meats, and other ingredients. This pool, however, is small, so the ingredients must be continually moved through it. Consequently, frying often requires constant stirring and turning with a spatula. Since the pan is curved, the spatula (ta-liu, ตะหลิว) has a curved scraping edge, and since it is used to dip up sauces, it is best if it is shaped like a shovel, with a solid blade (no perforations) and upturned margins.

One final piece of equipment found in Thai kitchens is a steamer (lung-theung, ลังถึง), which includes a wide pot with a high-domed lid and one or more trays that can be stacked up above the pot. The rims of the pot, the tray(s), and the lid all fit one another so as to hold steam reasonably well, and care should be taken in handling and storage lest the rims become deformed. Once steaming has begun, it should not be interrupted until the food is done; therefore, there should be an adequate supply of water in the pot. It is recommended that the pot be filled three-quarters full and then heated. While the water is heating, the food can be arranged in the steamer tray(s). When the water boils, the heat may be reduced; however, a good volume of steam should continue to be evolved. The tray(s) may then be fitted to the pot, covered with the lid, and the food allowed to steam. At the end of steaming, the lid is removed, then the trays are removed and separated, and the food is allowed to cool as necessary, The steamer may then be reloaded, first checking that there is adequate water in the pot.

The remainder of this introduction is a listing of some of the ingredients used in the recipes. The primary purpose is to specify the meaning of the English name used in the recipes for an ingredient by giving the name of that ingredient in Thai. It is hoped that this will assist in locating ingredients in Thai food stores and markets.

RICE

Rice, khao jaao, ข้าวเจ้า, the staple food in the central and southern parts of Thailand, is long-grained, nonglutinous rice. Uncooked grains are translucent; when cooked, the rice is white and fluffy.

Glutinous rice, khao niao, ข้าวเหนียว, also known as sticky rice, is the mainstay of the diet in the northern and northeastern regions of the country and is used in confections in all regions. Uncooked grains are starchy white in color.

Fermented rice, khao maak, ข้าวหมาก, is made by fermenting cooked glutinous rice and is sold as a sweet.

FLOUR

Rice flour, paeng khao jaao, แป้งข้าวเจ้า, is made from nonglutinous rice.

Glutionus rice flour, paeng khao niao, แป้งข้าวเหนียว, is made from glutinous rice.

Corn flour, paeng khao phoot, แป้งข้าวโพด, is a fine white flour made from corn.

Tapioca flour, paeng mun sampalang, แป้งมันสำปะหลัง, is made from tapioca, or cassava, tubers. When this or any of the other flours is used to thicken a sauce, it is first mixed well with a little water so that it will not lump in the sauce.

Wheat flour, paeng saa-lee, แป้งสาลี, may be general purpose flour unless cake flour is specified.

Tapioca pellets, sa-khu met lek, สาคูเม็ดเล็ก, are the tiny balls (about 2 mm. in diameter) made from tapioca, some used in sweets. They should be mixed with hot, but not scalding, water and kneaded, and then allowed to stand for a time covered with a damp cloth to permit the water to penetrate to the core.

NOODLES
Rice noodles, kui tiao, เส้นก๋วยเตี๋ยว, are flat white noodles made from rice flour and are cut into strips of three widths: **wide** (2-3 cm.), sen yai, เส้นใหญ่, **narrow** (about 5 mm.), sen lek, เส้นเล็ก, and **thin** (1-2 mm.), sen mee, เส้นหมี่, uncut fresh noodle sheets are sold in the market, as are fresh wide and narrow rice noodles. Thin noodles are available dried, and wide and narrow noodles may also be bought in this form. Dried noodles are soaked in water before use to soften them.

Vermicelli, khanom jeen, ขนมจีน, are thin, round noodles, also made from rice flour, and sold fresh in the form of wads that look like bird's nests. They should be eaten within a few days of being made, and it is a good practice to steam them after bringing them home from the market.

Egg noodles, ba mee, บะหมี่, are yellow noodles made from wheat flour, Directions for making them are given in the recipe for Ba Mee Nong Kai in this book. Small balls of this kind of noodle are available in the market.

Mung bean noodles, woon sen, วุ้นเส้น, are thread-like noodles made from mung bean flour. They are sold dried and are soaked in water before use. When cooked, they become transparent. High quality noodles maintain their integrity in soup better than do cheap ones.

SUGARS
Sugars, nam tan sai, น้ำตาลทราย, is granulated cane sugar. Colors range from white to reddish and textures from fine to coarse. Some people find the reddish sugar tastier than the more highly refined white. The cleanliness of sugars in the market varies so it is wise to inspect carefully for foreign matter before purchase.

Even so, some debris, such as tiny threads of cane, may remain and of sugar solutions when clarity is desired.

Brown sugar, nam tan sai daeng, น้ำตาลทรายแดง, is also a cane sugar but less refined than the above. Some brown sugars offered in the market are quite lumpy. While this makes accurate measurement difficult, such sugar is useable when it is to be dissolved, say, in a sauce.

Palm sugar, nam tan peep, น้ำตาลปีบ, is made from the sap of the sugar, or palmyra, palm, *Borassus flabellifera,* called taan in Thai, which has a very rough trunk and large, fan-shaped leaves. The sugar is a light golden brown paste with a distinctive flavor and fragrance. It is put up in five-gallon kerosene cans, called peep in Thai.

ANIMAL PRODUCTS

Fish sauce, nam pla, น้ำปลา, is a clear, brown liquid derived from a brew of fish or shrimp mixed with salt. It is sold in bottles and plastic jugs as well as in earthenware jars. High quality fish sauce has a fine aroma and taste. Fish sauce is placed on the table as a condiment at nearly every meal. either as is or mixed with sliced chillies and perhaps lemon juice.

Fermented fish, pla ra, ปลาร้า, is fish mixed with salt and roasted rice and brewed for a time: the longer, the better. It is the liquid, which is something like anchovy paste, that is used here. This may be obtained by placing some fermented fish in a strainer and pressing out the required amount.

Salted fish, pla khem, ปลาเค็ม, is dried, salted sea fish, such as pla insee, ปลา อินทรี. In the market, the seller will cut you a steak of the required thickness. This is slowly roasted for a time to bring out the aroma.

Dried fish, pla haeng, ปลาแห้ง, is a freshwater fish, such as serpent head, which is slit poen, gutted, and spread to dry in the sun.

Shrimp paste, ka-pi, กะปิ, is shrimp which are salted, perhaps brewed for a time, allowed to dry in the sun, then ground and worked with the addition of moisture into a fine-textured puce paste, which is fragrant and slightly salty.

Dried shrimp, koong haeng, กุ้งแห้ง, are small shrimp which have been dried in the sun. The quality product is plump orange and whitish shrimp with a minimum of debris.

Mackerel, pla too, ปลาทู, is a small saltwater fish, *Rastrelliger chrysozonus* (Scombridae). Steamed mackerel in small woven trays are sold in food shops nearly everywhere in the country; **fresh mackerel,** pla too sot, ปลาทูสด, are available at the fishmonger's in the market.

Sea mussels, hoi malaeng phuu, หอยแมลงภู่, have a dark brown and iridescent green shell and a bright orange body inside. Shelled mussels may be bought at the market.

Sea bass, pla kaphong, ปลากะพง, is a general name for fish of the sea bass and sea perch families.

Red snapper, pla daeng, ปลาแดง, is the saltwater fish, *Lutjanus annularis* (Lutianidae).

Catfish, pla dook, ปลาดุก, is a small freshwater catfish, *Clarias batrachus* (Clariidae).

Climbing perch, pla maw, ปลาหมอ, is the freshwater fish, *Anabas testudineus* (Anabantidae).

Featherback, pla krai, ปลากราย, is the freshwater fish, *Notopterus chitala*.

Serpent head, pla chawn, ปลาช่อน, is the freshwater fish, *Ophiocephalus striatus.*

Crisp fried catfish, pla dook foo, ปลาดุกฟู, is a catfish which has been washed, cleaned, and roasted or steamed until done. It is then split open and the bones removed. The meat is broken up with the tines of a fork, then fried in an abundance of hot oil until crisp, fluffy, and golden brown.

Scraped fish meat, neua pla khoot, เนื้อปลาขูด, can be purchased in the market or can be obtained by skinning a fish such as a featherback and then scraping the meat from the fish with the edge of a spoon, being careful to remove any small bones. The meat can then be worked into uniform smooth consistency by pounding in a mortar. Dipping the pestle in water from time to time helps keep the meat from clinging to it.

Eggs, khai, ไข่, may be either hen's eggs, khai kai, ไข่ไก่, or duck eggs, khai pet, ไข่เป็ด, unless specified in the recipe. Traditionally, duck eggs have been preferred.

Salted eggs, khai khem, ไข่เค็ม, are duck eggs preserved by soaking in brine for a month or so.

Pork belly, mu sam chun, หมูสามชั้น, is bacon-cut pork, with alternating layers of red meat, fat, and skin.

Fermented pork, naem, แหนม, is chopped pork mixed with thin strips of pig skin and fermented for a couple of days. The longer it ferments, the sourer it becomes. Traditionally, fermented pork has been made up into finger-sized rolls, each with a chilli or two inserted, and wrapped in banana leaf. In recent years, fermented pork in rolls of various sizes packaged in plastic have been put on the market by a number of provisioners.

Soup stock, nam soup, น้ำซุป, made from chicken is preferred in Thai cooking. While plain water can substitute, and while the instant chicken broth cubes and pastes marketed by various food manufacturers are certainly fast and convenient, it might be interesting to make up this stock: Chop 1 1/2 kg. chicken bones and scrap into 3-4 inch long pieces, place in a pot with 10 cups water and allow to stand 30 minutes. Peel 2 white radishes, cut in half lengthwise and add to pot. Wash 3 celery plants and 3 garlic plants, remove the roots, coil the plants together, tie into a bundle, and add to pot, together with 5 bay leaves and 2 tbsp. salt. Heat to boiling, simmer over low heat for 1-1 1/2 hours, and then strain through cheesecloth.

BEANS AND BEAN PRODUCTS

Soybean curd, tao huu, เต้าหู้, is made up salted and unsalted in solid and soft forms. The solid curd has a cheesy consistency and is sold in blocks about four inches square. The blocks of the unsalted curd are white while those of the salted,

yellow soybean curd, tao huu leuang, เต้าหู้เหลือง, are yellow on the outside and off-white inside. The solid curd is used in fried dishes. The **soft white bean curd**, tao huu khaao chanit awn, เต้าหู้ขาวชนิดอ่อน, is cut into bricks for sale and is used in soups.

Fermented bean curd, tao huu yee, เต้าหู้ยี้, is small cakes of the solid curd put up in a red pickling solution. It is sold in the market both by the cake and by the jar.

Fermented soybeans, tao jiao, เต้าเจี้ยว, is a brew of soybeans and salt.

Soybean paste, tao jiao nam, เต้าเจี้ยวน้ำ, is a preparation made with fermented soybeans and flour.

Soy sauces, see-ieu, ซีอิ๊ว, used in these recipes are of the Chinese, rather than the Japanese, type.

Light soy sauce, see-ieu khao, ซีอิ๊วขาว, is a clear brown liquid used in much the same way that fish sauce is.

Dark soy sauce, see-ieu dum, ซีอิ๊วดำ, is opaque, black, viscous, and sweet.

Black beans, thua dum, ถั่วดำ, are a small dark bean sold dry and used in sweets.

Mung beans, thua khiao, ถั่วเขียว, are small yellow beans with green shells. The shelled bean is used in sweets and the whole bean is sprouted, giving bean sprouts, thua ngawk, ถั่วงอก.

String beans, thua fuk yao, ถั่วฝักยาว, also known as yardlong beans, have pods up to 60 cm. long. These are eaten both fresh and cooked and are at their best when young and slender.

Winged bean, thua phu, ถั่วพู, bears a pod which in cross section looks like a rectangle that has a fringe-like extension at each corner, the "wings" of the bean.

HERBS AND SPICES

Ginger, khing, ขิง, *Zingiber officinale*, grows from an underground stems, or rhisome. Mature ginger stems are buff colored; **young or fresh ginger**, khing awn, ขิงอ่อน, is white and is eaten fresh and pickled as well as cooked.

Galangal, kha, ข่า, *Alphinia galangal*, is a larger and lighter-colored relative of ginger and has its own distinctive taste.

Ginger

Krachai

Galangal

Lemon grass

Garlic

Shallot

Onion

Cinnamon

Cumin

Cardamoms

Pepper

Bay leaf

Coconut

Ma-euk

Coriander

Chillies

Ma-kheua phuang

Ma-kheua pro

Long eggplant

Lemon

Kaffir lime

Turmeric

Madan

Ripe Tamarind

Spring onion

Krachai, กระชาย, *Kaempferia panduratum,* grows bunches of slender and short yellow brown tuberous roots and is used in fish dishes.

Turmeric, kha-min, ขมิ้น, *Curcuma longa,* is a small ginger with brown rhisomes. Inside, the flesh is a bright carrot orange. An important use is as a coloring agent.

Lemon grass, ta-khrai, ตะไคร้, *Cymbopgon citratus,* is an aromatic grey green grass. The bases of the stems are used in cookery.

Garlic, kra-thiam, กระเทียม, *Allium sativum,* is used both by the clove and by the entire bulb. The dry papery skin and the central core should be removed from bulbs. Cloves are often crushed by hitting with a spatula or the side of a knife blade and then the skins are picked out. **Pickled garlic**, kra-thiam dawng, กระเทียม ดอง, are wonderfully flavorful and can be bought by the bulb or by the jar in the market.

Shallot, hawm lek, หอมเล็ก, or hawm daeng, หอมแดง, *Allium ascalonicum,* is the zesty small red onion favored in Thai cooking.

Onion, hawm hua yai, หอมหัวใหญ่, *Allium cepa,* has light colored bulbs that are larger and milder than those of the shallot.

Cinnamon, ope-choey, อบเชย, *Cinnamomum spp.,* is the bark of a number of species of trees in this genus, classified in the laurel family. The types that grow in Southeast Asia are known in commerce as cassias. The barks, which are generally reddish-brown, after being peeled off from around the branch, tend to roll themselves back up, and so have a scroll-like appearance. For retail sale in Thai markets, the bark is cut into strips about 1 cm. across and 8-10 cm. long, and such strips are the basis for the measurements given in the recipes. Before use, the bark should be roasted to bring out its aroma.

Cha-em, ชะเอม, is sold in herbal medicine shops in the form of strips of yellowish, light cane-like wood which is very sweet. This is probably the root of *Glycyrrhiza glabra,* from which licorice is made.

Cloves, kan phluu, กานพลู, are the very fragrant tack-like flower buds of the tree *Caryophyllus aromaticus,* thought to be native to insular Southeast Asia.

Cumin, yee-ra, ยี่หร่า, *Cuminium cyminun,* has elongated yellow brown seeds about 5 mm. in length, which are ridged longitudinally and often have a seed stalk attached. They are roasted before use to heighten their fragrance.

Sesame, nga, งา, *Sesamum indicum,* has small oval seeds which are white and have dark hulls. They are usually sold hulled.

Cardamoms, luke kra-wan, ลูกกระวาน, *Amomum krevanh,* appear like minia-ture unhusked coconuts. The off-white, bulb-shaped capsules reach about 1 cm. in length and slightly more than this in diameter. Inside is a densely-packed cluster of angular, dark brown seeds, which are aromatic and have a slightly hot taste.

Bay leaf, bai kra-wan, ใบกระวาน, is an elliptical leaf about 7 cm. long, grey green on the bottom, having a brownish cast on the top, which is sold dried in the market.

Coriander, phak chee, ผักชี, *Coriandrum sativum,* is of the parsley family. The leaves and stems are eaten fresh and used frequently as a garnish. The root and the seeds are ingredients in many dishes. The root is taken from the fresh plant. The seeds, which are roughly spherical, 2-4 cm. in diameter, and range in color from off-white to brown, have a pleasant taste and fragrance. They can be bought in the market. It is better to roast and grind seeds immediately before use than to buy ground coriander seed.

Sweet basil, maenglak, แมงลัก, is a bright light green plant with a tangy taste.

Sweet basil, horapha, โหระพา, is an attractive plant with deep green leaves and often reddish stems. It has a taste reminiscent of anise.

Pepper, phrik thai, พริกไทย, *Piper nigrum,* produces berries, which, when ripe, are dried and ground with the skins on to give black pepper, or with the skins off to give white pepper. The most widely available form in Thailand is white pepper.

Chillies, phrik, พริก, *Capsicum annuum,* of several varieties are available in Thai-land. As they ripen, they change color from green to red and become hotter. Fully ripe fruits are dried in the sun to give **dried chillies**, phrik haeng, พริกแห้ง and these are pounded for **ground dried chilli**, phrik pone, พริกป่น.

Hot chillies, phrik khee nuu, พริกขี้หนู, are the hottest type and also the smallest,

Chinese cabbage

Celery

Kale

Chinese mustard green

Swamp cabbage

String beans

Bitter gourd

Sponge gourd

Wax gourd

Coral tree leaves

Pumpkin

Cha-phloo

White radish

being only about a centimeter long.

Jasmine, ma-lee, มะลิ, *Jasminum sambac,* has very fragrant white blossoms. The flowers are floated in water to scent it.

Pandanus leaf, bai toey, ใบเตย, *Pandanus odorus,* the long, bright green leaf of a small palm and is used in making sweets.

Kra-dung-ngaa, กระดังงา, *Canangium odoratum,* also called ilang-ilang or ylang-ylang has large green yellow flowers used in scenting sweets.

Saffron, yaa frun, หญ้าฝรั่น, is the stigmas from the flower of *Crocus sativus* and is used as a coloring agent. Tumeric may be substituted.

FRUITS AND VEGETABLES

Eggplant, ma-kheua, มะเขือ, *Solanum spp.,* are eaten with nam phrik. There are a number of types, ranging in size from that of a ping-pong ball down to that of a marble, in shape from that of an egg to that of a flattened sphere, and in color from green and white to yellow. One small type is called **ma-kheua pro**, มะเขือเปราะ.

Ma-kheua phuang, มะเขือพวง, *Solanum torvum,* grow in clusters and, when yet unripe, look like large peas.

Ma-euk, มะอึก, *Solanum ferox,* is an eggplant having a furry fruit with a sour taste. The hairs are scraped off before use.

Long eggplant, ma-kheua yaao, มะเขือยาว, has a long green fruit used to make types of nam phrik, It is also cut into long, thin slices, mixed with egg, and fried.

Banana, Nam Wa variety, kluai nam wa, กล้วยน้ำว้า, *Musa sapientum,* probably the most popular eating banana among the nearly thirty varieties found in Thailand, has short oblong fruits that become a pale yellow as they ripen. The leaf, bai tawng, ใบตอง, of this variety is used in Glutinous Rice Wrapped in Banana Leaf. Wrapping goes more easily if the sections are torn and allowed to stand overight before wrapping.

Bael fruit, matoom, มะตูม, *Aegle marmelos,* has bright orange-red flesh with seeds arranged in a circle about the core. The fruits are cut into thin circular slices and dried. The slices are roasted and then steeped in hot water to make a fragrant tea.

Coconut, ma-phraao, มะพร้าว, Cocos nucifera, is found nearly everywhere people have settled in all parts of the country and its production is important to the economy. The use of coconut milk in curries is a hallmark of Thai cooking. The meat of ripe nuts is scraped either by hand or by machine. The grated coconut is placed in a basin and mixed with a certain amount of warm water. The coconut is then picked up in the hand, help over a second container, and squeezed to press out the **coconut milk**, ka-thi, กะทิ, A finemeshed strainer should be positioned below the hand during squeezing to catch any meat that falls. Many cooks add a little salt to the water or the milk.

Coconut cream, hua ka-thi, หัวกะทิ, can be obtained by mixing a little warm water with the grated coconut and collecting the required amount of cream on the first squeezing. Following this, water can be added again and the grated coconut can be squeezed a second and a third time to obtain a less rich milk, which is kept separate from the cream. Alternatively, the full amount of warm water may be mixed with the grated coconut. After squeezing, the liquid is allowed to stand for a time, and then the cream is skimmed from top with a spoon.

Fastidious cooks scrape mature brown coconuts themselves by hand and coconut thus grated is usually pure white. In the market, however, the work is done with a machine that accepts chunks of coconut cut from the shell and usually a thin layer of shell still adheres to the meat. As a result, the grated coconut sold in the market is flecked with tiny brown particles of shell. This is useable for making coconut milk but is unacceptable when the grated coconut itself is to be used, for example, as a topping for a sweet. For such purposes, the recipes specify **white grated coconut**, ma-phraao khaao, มะพร้าวขาว, which is also available in the market.

For the sake of efficiency in extracting coconut milk, grated coconut is quite fine, but in making sweets, a coarser cut is sometimes desired. This **shredded coconut**, ma-phraao theun theuk khoot kradaai jeen, มะพร้าวทีนทึกขูดกระต่ายจีน, is sold in the market and is obtained by using a special scraper. This lacking, the top of a soft drink bottle might be used to scrape threads of coconut meat.

For those who wish to avoid the bother scraping and squeezing, ready-made coconut milk is offered by food processors. This can be used in the recipes simply by measuring out the amount specified. In recipes which distinguish coconut cream from coconut milk, coconut cream is approximated by the ready-made coconut milk used full strength right from the container, while coconut milk may be approximated by mixing one part of the ready-made product with one part water.

Lemon, ma-naao, มะนาว, *Citrus acida*, also called lime, has small spherical fruits which are green or yellow.

Kaffir lime, ma-kruut, มะกรูด, *Citrus hystrix*, has green fruits with wrinkled skin. The rind and the leaves are used in cookery.

Madan, มะดัน, *Garcinia schomburgkiana*, has avocado green fruits about 2 inches long which are sour.

Rakam, ระกำ, *Zalacca wallichiana*, is a palm which bears clusters of bright red fruit. Beneath the spiny red skin is a large seed surrounded by brownish flesh which may be sweet or sour.

Star gooseberry, ma-yom, มะยม, *Phyllanthus distichus*, has cannister-like small, pale green fruits with pithy flesh that is quite sour.

Tamarind, ma-khaam, มะขาม, *Tamarindus indica,* is a tree which bears tan pods inside of which are bean-like hard brown seeds surrounded by sticky flesh. The tan pod shell can be removed easily. **Ripe tamarind**, ma-khaam piak, มะขาม-เปียก, is the flesh, seeds, and veins, of several fruit pressed together in the hand to form a wad.

Tamarind juice, nam ma-khaam piak, น้ำมะขามเปียก, is obtained by mixing some of the ripe fruit with water and squeezing out the juice. The immature fruit and the young leaves and flowers are also used, all to give a sour taste. There are also sweet tamarinds which are a delight to eat and command a high price.

Mushrooms, het, เห็ด, of many types are available fresh. The most common is the **rice straw mushroom**, het faang, เห็ดฟาง.

Chinese mushroom, het hawm, เห็ดหอม, is available in the market.

Spring onion, ton hawm, ต้นหอม, *Allium fistulosum*, also called green onion or scallion, has leaves that are circular in cross section. These are much used as a garnish. The bases of the plant are frequently served on the side of one-dish meals, such as fried rice, or placed on the salad plate.

Garlic plant, ton kra-thiam, ต้นกระเทียม, *Allium sativum*, is the young plant picked before the bulb has formed. The leaves are flat and folded lengthwise.

Chinese leek, ton kui chai, ต้นกุยช่าย, *Allium tuberosum*, has fairly thick, narrow, flat leaves which are eaten with fried noodle dishes such as Phad Thai.

Celery, kheun chai, ขึ้นฉ่าย, *Apium graveolens*, also called celeriac, turniprooted celery, or Chinese soup celery, has very small stalks (only a few millimeters across) and a very strong flavor.

White radish, phak kaat hua, ผักกาดหัว, or hua chai thao, หัวไชเท้า, *Raphanus sativus* (longpinnatus variety), also called Chinese radish, has a long, cylindrical root that looks like a hefty white carrot.

Chinese cabbage, phak kaat khaao, ผักกาดขาว, *Brassica campestris* (pekinensis variety), has thin, light green leaves and broad, flat, and thin leaf ribs which form an elongaged, rather than a spherical, head.

Kale, phak kha-naa, ผักคะน้า, *Brassica oleracea* (acephala variety), has leathery grey green leaves on thick stalks. Stalk lovers buy the large variety, while those partial to the leaves get the dwarf variety.

Chinese mustard green, phak kwaang toong, ผักกวางตุ้ง, *Brassica campestris* (chinensis variety), has dark green oval leaves on thick fleshy stalks.

Swamp cabbage, phak boong, ผักบุ้ง, *Ipomoea aquatica*, also called water convolvulus, water spinach, or aquatic morning glory, has hollow stems and roughly triangular leaves. The Thai veriety has delicate dark green leaves and deep red stalks while the Chinese is thicker, larger, and lighter green. The tender tips of the stems are eaten fresh or cooked.

Water mimosa, phak kra-chet, ผักกระเฉด, *Neptunia oleracea*, has small dark green compound leaves and a smooth green stem encased in a white foam-like material, which is stripped off before use.

Bitter gourd, ma-ra, มะระ, *Momordica charantia*, also called bitter cucumber, carilla fruit, or balsam pear, is an oblong fruit, pointed at one end, which has a handsome pale green surface covered with an irregular pattern of ridges. There are also small dark green varieties. The young leaves and shoots are also eaten. All are bitter to the taste.

Bottle gourd, nam tao, น้ำเต้า, *Lagenaria leucantha*, has a rounded body from which arises a straight, narrow neck. The young green gourd is used as food.

Sponge gourd, buap liam, บวบเหลี่ยม, *Luffa acutangula*, also called vegetable gourd or Chinese oka, is oblong, pointed, and dark green and has sharp longitudinal ridges.

Wax gourd, fuk khiao, ฟักเขียว, *Benincasa hispida*, also called white gourd or Chinese preserving melon, is oblong and light green to white. The ends are rounded and the flesh is solid and white.

Cucumber, taeng kwaa, แตงกวา, *Cucumis sativus*, has short fruits about 8 cm. long which are crispiest while still green and white, before yellowing. A larger type, taeng raan, แตงร้าน, are also eaten.

Pumpkin, fuk thawng, ฟักทอง, *Cucurbita spp.*, also called winter squash, has very rough surfaced fruits with dark green to sorrel skin and yellow flesh. Fruits about 6 inches across are used for Custard Steamed in Pumpkin. For other dishes, you can have the vendor cut a piece of the required size.

Water chestnut, haeo, แห้ว, is the tuber of certain kinds of sedges. The skin is dark and the crunchy meat inside is off-white.

Cha-phloo, ชะพลู, *Piper sarmentosum*, is a creeper with aromatic glossy dark green leaves which resemble those of the betel vine.

Coral tree leaves, bai thawng laang, ใบทองหลาง, *Erythrina Variegatyta*, have three ovate leaflets and are eaten as a green.

Cha-ohm, ชะอม, *Acacia insuavis*, has feathery leaves which are used in some curries and also are mixed with egg and fried.

Gord gourd, phak dumleung, ผักตำลึง, *Coccina indica*, is a small vine bearing a cucumber-like fruit which turns red when ripe. The tips of the vines and the young leaves are used in soups and as a fresh green.

Hog plum leaves, bai ma-kawk, ใบมะกอก, *Spondias pinnata*, when young are light green with a reddish tinge and have a tangy taste that goes well with meat dishes.

Kra-thin, กระถิน, *Leucaena glauca*, is a small tree of the bean family. The young leaves and pods are tender and are eaten fresh.

Indian Pennywort, bua boke, บัวบก, *Centella asiatica*, is a creeping herb with succulent leaves and stems.

Phak wan, ผักหวาน, *Melientha suavis*, is a forest tree whose young leaves and flowers are much relished.

Yaw, ยอ, *Morinda citrifolia*, has large dark green leaves used in making Hor Mok.

PREPARED SPICE MIXTURES

Anise seed powder, phong pha-loh, ผงพะโล้, is a prepared mixture of spices, among which is star anise, poi-kak, โป๊ยกั๊ก, *Illicium verum*.

Curry Powder, phong karee, ผงกะหรี่, is a prepared mixture of spices such as tumeric, coriander seed, ginger, cloves, cinnamon, mustard, cardamon, cumin, chilli, and salt. Each brand has its own character depending on the ingredients used.

Roasted chilli curry paste, phril kaeng or nam phrik kaeng khua, พริกแกง or น้ำพริกแกงคั่ว, is a prepared mixture containing dried chillies, shallots and garlic as well as other ingredients, all roasted and pounded and them mixed with fish sauce to give them the consistency of a paste. Vendors stock a number of types, each for a certain kind of curry.

THE BEST OF
THAI CUISINE

Stewed Beef : เนื้อตุ๋น

Stewed Beef

INGREDIENTS:

½ kg beef shank
10 cups water
1 cm length of cinnamon, broken into
  small pieces
½ inch length of galangal
3 coriander roots
2 tbsp. light soy sauce

1 tbsp. dark soy sauce
2 tsp. salt
1 bay leaf (krawan leaf)
2 celery plants
200 grams lettuce, swamp cabbage,
  or bean sprouts
2 tbsp. fried garlic

PREPARATION:

- Wash meat, cut into 1 inch cubes, place in pot.
- Add water, cinnamon, coriander roots, light soy sauce, dark soy sauce, salt, and bay leaf.
- Heat to a boil, then cover, reduce heat, and simmer until the meat is tender. (If using an ordinary pot, this will be 3-4 hours. With a pressure cooker, use only 2 cups of water and cook for 25 minutes, then remove from heat, allow to cool, open lid, and add 3 cups boiled water.) Season to taste and bring to a boil once again.
- Blanch swamp cabbage, cut into 1 inch pieces, and place in bottom of serving bowl. Place stewed beef on the vegetable, sprinkle with coarsely cut coriander and celery, fried garlic, and pepper, and serve with rice or noodles and pickled chilli pepper, made by boiling 1 chilli and 5 cloves garlic until soft then pounding and mixing with ¼ cup vinegar.

เนื้อตุ๋น

เครื่องปรุง					
เนื้อเอ็นน่อง	$\frac{1}{2}$	กิโลกรัม	ใบกระวาน	1	ใบ
อบเชยชิ้นเล็ก ๆ ขนาด	1	ซม.	ขึ้นฉ่าย	2	ต้น
ข่าชิ้นขนาด	$\frac{1}{2}$	นิ้ว	ผักกาดหอมหรือผักบุ้งจีน หรือ		
รากผักชี	3	ราก	ถั่วงอกก็ได้	200	กรัม
ซีอิ๊วขาว	2	ช้อนโต๊ะ	กระเทียมเจียว	2	ช้อนโต๊ะ
ซีอิ๊วดำ	1	ช้อนชา			

Sweet and Sour Spareribs

INGREDIENTS:

300 grams spareribs, cut into 1½ inch lengths and marinated 2-3 hours in 1 tbsp. light soy sauce, 1 tsp. ground pepper, 1 tsp. salt, 1 tbsp. corn flour, and 1 tbsp. Chinese wine

¼ cup chilli, sliced diagonally
½ cup pineapple, sliced into cubes
½ cup onion rings
¼ cup shredded pickled ginger
½ cup tomato, cut into quarters

INGREDIENTS FOR THE SWEET AND SOUR SAUCE:

½ cup tomato catsup
¼ cup shredded fresh young ginger

1 tbsp. vinegar
1 tbsp. sugar
½ tbsp. salt

½ tsp. pepper
3 cups soup stock

PREPARATION:

- Fry marinated spareribs until golden brown in ½ cup cooking oil then remove from pan and drain.
- Mix the ingredients for the sweet and sour sauce in a pot, heat to boiling, then simmer about 15 minutes. Strain the sauce to remove any lumps. When ready to serve:
- Place the fried pork ribs on a platter.
- Heat ¼ cup oil in a frying pan until very hot. Put chilli, pineapple, tomato, onion, and ginger into the pan and fry until done. Add 1 cup of the sweet and sour sauce. In a bowl, mix 2 tbsp. corn flour with 3 tbsp. water, and add this to the mixture in the pan to thicken it, then spoon over the spareribs.

กระดูกหมูเปรี้ยวหวาน

เครื่องปรุง

กระดูกหมูอ่อนตัดเป็นท่อน ๆ
1$\frac{1}{2}$ นิ้ว 300 กรัม (หมักกับ
ซีอิ๊วขาว 1 ช้อนโต๊ะ พริกไทย
1 ช้อนชา น้ำตาลทราย 1 ช้อน
โต๊ะ เกลือ 1 ช้อนชา แป้งข้าว
โพด 1 ช้อนโต๊ะ เหล้าจีน 1
ช้อนโต๊ะ หมักไว้ประมาณ
2-3 ชั่วโมง

พริกชี้ฟ้าหั่นแฉลบ ๆ	$\frac{1}{2}$ ถ้วย
สับปะรด หั่นสี่เหลี่ยม	$\frac{1}{2}$ ถ้วย
หอมใหญ่หั่นแว่น	$\frac{1}{2}$ ถ้วย
ขิงดองหั่นฝอย	$\frac{1}{4}$ ถ้วย
มะเขือเทศผ่าสี่	$\frac{1}{2}$ ถ้วย

เครื่องปรุงซอสเปรี้ยวหวาน

ซอสมะเขือเทศ	$\frac{1}{2}$ ถ้วย	พริกชี้ฟ้าเขียวแดงหั่นแฉลบ	4	เม็ด
ขิงอ่อนหั่นฝอย	$\frac{1}{4}$ ถ้วย	เกลือ	$\frac{1}{2}$	ช้อนโต๊ะ
น้ำส้มสายชู	1 ช้อนโต๊ะ	พริกไทย	$\frac{1}{2}$	ช้อนโต๊ะ
น้ำตาลทราย	1 ช้อนโต๊ะ	น้ำซุป	3	ถ้วย

Shrimp in Sauce : กุ้งผัดกับซอส

Shrimp in Sauce

INGREDIENTS:

300 grams shelled shrimp
4 large tomatoes
1 tbsp. finely chopped fresh ginger
2 tbsp. tomato catsup
1 tbsp. corn flour
4 tbsp. water

1 tsp. finely chopped garlic
2 tbsp. finely chopped spring onion
1 tbsp. sherry
1 tbsp. chilli sauce
4 tbsp. cooking oil

PREPARATION:

- Slice the tomatoes into quarters
- In a bowl, mix the catsup, corn flour, and water together until smooth.
- Place oil in frying pan and heat. When hot, add the ginger, garlic, and spring onion and fry until fragrant. Add the shrimp and fry about 2 minutes before adding the tomatoes, then reduce heat and stir to mix for 30 seconds.
- Add sherry, chilli sauce, and catsup and flour mixture, stirring constantly to prevent burning. Continue cooking over low heat until the sauce thickens, then spoon onto serving plate.

กุ้งผัดกับซอส

เครื่องปรุง					
กุ้งแกะเปลือก	300	กรัม	กระเทียมสับละเอียด	1	ช้อนชา
มะเขือเทศ	4	ผลใหญ่	ต้นหอมหั่นละเอียด	2	ช้อนโต๊ะ
ขิงสดสับละเอียด	1	ช้อนโต๊ะ	เหล้าเชอรี่	1	ช้อนโต๊ะ
ซอสมะเขือเทศ	2	ช้อนโต๊ะ	ซอสพริกชนิดเผ็ดกลาง	1	ช้อนโต๊ะ
แป้งข้าวโพด	1	ช้อนโต๊ะ	น้ำมัน	4	ช้อนโต๊ะ
น้ำ	4	ช้อนโต๊ะ			

Pork Fried with Chillies, Ginger, and String Beans

INGREDIENTS FOR CHILLI PASTE:

3 dried chillies	1 tbsp. lemon grass	1 tsp. salt
7 shallots	5 pepper corns	1 tsp. shrimp paste
2 garlic bulbs	1 tsp. coriander root	2 tbsp. ground dried
1 tsp. galangal	1 tsp. kaffir lime rind	shrimp

OTHER INGREDIENTS:

300 grams pork	2 tbsp. cooking oil	1 tbsp. fish sauce
200 grams string beans	1 tbsp. palm sugar	

PREPARATION:

- Place chilli paste ingredients in mortar and pound until thoroughly ground and mixed.
- Wash pork, cut into long, thin slices, and marinate in 1 tsp. fish sauce.
- Wash string beans, cut into 1 inch lengths, boil until just cooked, and remove from water.
- Heat oil in a frying pan, fry the pork until done, then remove the pork from the pan and set aside.
- Put the chilli paste in the pan and fry until fragrant, then add the pork, sugar, fish sauce, and string beans. Stir to mix. When done, scoop up onto serving plate.

ผัดพริกขิงหมู กับ ถั่วฝักยาว

เครื่องปรุง

พริกแห้ง	3	เม็ด	รากผักชี	1	ช้อนชา
หัวหอม	7	หัว	ผิวมะกรูด	1	ช้อนชา
กระเทียม	2	หัว	เกลือ	1	ช้อนชา
ข่า	1	ช้อนชา	กะปิ	1	ช้อนชา
ตะไคร้	1	ช้อนโต๊ะ	กุ้งแห้งป่น	2	ช้อนโต๊ะ
พริกไทย	5	เม็ด			

เครื่องปรุงอื่น

เนื้อหมูหั่นชิ้นเล็ก ๆ	300	กรัม	น้ำตาลปีบ	1	ช้อนโต๊ะ
ถั่วฝักยาวหั่น 1 ชิ้น	200	กรัม	น้ำปลา	1	ช้อนโต๊ะ
น้ำมัน	2	ช้อนโต๊ะ			

Sweet, Sour, and Salty Spareribs : ซี่โครงหมูสามรส

Sweet, Sour, and Salty Spareribs *(See Khrong Moo Sam Rot)*

INGREDIENTS:

1 kg spareribs	½ cup pineapple juice	10 bite-size pineapple
3 tbsp. flour	1 tbsp. light soy sauce	chunks
2 tsp. salt	1 tbsp. brown sugar	cooking oil
1 tsp. pepper	2 tbsp. vinegar	

PREPARATION:

- Chop spare-ribs into 2 inch lengths, bread in mixture of flour, salt, and pepper, fry until golden brown, and drain.
- Place spareribs in a pot with the pineapple juice, vinegar, sugar, and light soy sauce and cook over low heat until the spareribs are done, stirring to prevent sticking.
- Place the spareribs on a platter with pineapple chunks. Serve with rice.

ซี่โครงหมูสามรส

เครื่องปรุง

ซี่โครงหมูชนิดมีเนื้อติดมาก ๆ	1	กิโลกรัม	ซีอิ๊วขาว	1	ช้อนโต๊ะ
แป้งสาลี	3	ช้อนโต๊ะ	น้ำตาลทรายแดง	1	ช้อนโต๊ะ
เกลือ	2	ช้อนชา	น้ำส้ม	2	ช้อนโต๊ะ
น้ำสับปะรด	½	ถ้วย	สับปะรดหั่นชิ้นขนาดคำ	10	ชิ้น
พริกไทย	1	ช้อนชา	น้ำมันสำหรับทอด		

Phanaeng Kai *(Chicken Curry)*

INGREDIENTS FOR SPICE MIXTURE:

5 small dried chillies	1 tsp. lemon grass	1 tsp. salt
5 shallots	½ tbsp. kaffir lime rind	1 tsp. shrimp paste
10 garlic cloves	1 tsp. coriander root	
1 tsp. galangal	5 pepper corns	

Place all ingredients in a mortar and pound until ground and mixed thoroughly.

OTHER INGREDIENTS:

300 grams chicken (pork or beef may also be used)	1 tbsp. fish sauce
	2 stems of sweet basil (horapha)
250 grams grated coconut	1 tbsp. sugar
2 kaffir lime leaves	1 tbsp. cooking oil

PREPARATION:

- Add ½ cup water to the coconut and squeeze out 1 cup coconut milk.
- Cut chicken into long thin pieces, fry until just done, and remove from pan.
- Heat the oil in pan and fry spice mixture. When fragrant, add coconut milk to prevent drying out, and cook over low heat until oil appears on surface.
- Add the chicken, mix in, then add kaffir lime leaves and sugar and fish sauce to taste. Add remaining coconut milk, simmer over low heat until the chicken is tender and the curry thick, then add sweet basil leaves and remove from heat.
- Dip into serving bowl and garnish with sprigs of sweet basil.

If beef is used, the slices of meat must be simmered in coconut milk until tender before being added to the spice mixture.

พะแนงไก่

เครื่องปรุง

เนื้อไก่ หั่นเป็นชิ้นเล็กยาว	300	กรัม	น้ำปลา	1	ช้อนโต๊ะ
มะพร้าว	250	กรัม	ใบโหระพา	2	กิ่ง
น้ำ	½	ถ้วย	น้ำตาล	1	ช้อนโต๊ะ
ใบมะกรูด	2	ใบ	น้ำมัน	1	ช้อนโต๊ะ

เครื่องน้ำพริกพะแนง (จะทำแกงคั่วหรือห่อหมกก็ได้)

พริกแห้ง	5	เม็ดเล็ก	ผิวมะกรูดหั่นละเอียด	½	ช้อนโต๊ะ
หอม	5	หัว	รากผักชี	1	ช้อนชา
กระเทียม	10	กลีบ	พริกไทย	5	เม็ด
ข่า	1	ช้อนชา	เกลือ	1	ช้อนชา
ตะไคร้	1	ช้อนชา	กะปิ	1	ช้อนชา

Kaeng Phed Kai, Kaeng Khiao Wan Kai *(Thai Chicken Curries)*

INGREDIENTS FOR CHILLI PASTE:

5 dried chillies (Kaeng Phed) or
20 hot chillies (Kaeng Khiao Wan)
10 cloves garlic
1 tsp. sliced galangal
1 tbsp. sliced lemon grass
½ tsp. sliced kaffir lime rind

1 tsp. coriander root
5 pepper corns
1 tbsp. roasted coriander seeds
1 tsp. roasted cumin seeds
1 tsp. salt
1 tsp. shrimp paste

For Kaeng Phed use dried chillies; for Kaeng Khiao Wan, fresh hot chillies.

OTHER INGREDIENTS:

300 grams chicken
250 grams grated coconut
100 grams eggplant (makheua phuang)
2 kaffir lime leaves

2 stems of sweet basil (horapha)
1½-2 tbsp. fish sauce
1 tbsp. palm sugar
1 tbsp. cooking oil

PREPARATION:

- Cut chicken into long, thin slices.
- Add 2 cups water to coconut and squeeze out 1 cup coconut cream and 1½ cups coconut milk.
- Place chilli paste ingredients in a mortar and pound until ground and mixed thoroughly. Fry chilli paste with oil until fragrant, reduce heat, add coconut cream a little at a time, and cook with stirring until coconut cream begins to have an oily sheen.
- Add the chicken and torn kaffir lime leaves and cook a short time, then dip curry into a pot, add the coconut milk and the sugar and fish sauce to taste, and heat. When boiling, add the makheua phuang. When the meat is done, add the sweet basil and remove from heat.

Pork or beef can be used in place of chicken.

แกงเผ็ดและแกงเขียวหวานไก่

เครื่องปรุงอื่น

เนื้อไก่หั่นเป็นชิ้นเล็ก ๆ ตาม		ใบโหระพา	2 กิ่ง
ยาว	300 กรัม	น้ำปลา	$1\frac{1}{2}$ -2 ช้อนโต๊ะ
มะพร้าว	250 กรัม	น้ำตาลปีบ	1 ช้อนโต๊ะ
มะเขือพวง	100 กรัม	น้ำมัน	1 ช้อนโต๊ะ
ใบมะกรูด	2 ใบ		

เครื่องปรุงน้ำพริก

พริกแห้ง	5	เม็ดเล็ก	รากผักชี	1	ช้อนชา
หรือพริกขี้หนู	20	เม็ด	พริกไทย	5	เม็ด
หัวหอม	5	หัว	ลูกผักชีคั่ว	1	ช้อนโต๊ะ
กระเทียม	10	กลีบ	ยี่หร่าคั่ว	1	ช้อนชา
ข่าหั่นละเอียด	1	ช้อนชา	เกลือ	1	ช้อนชา
ตะไคร้ซอย	1	ช้อนโต๊ะ	กะปิ	1	ช้อนชา
ผิวมะกรูด	$\frac{1}{2}$	ช้อนชา			

(แกงเผ็ดใช้พริกแห้ง แกงเขียวหวานใช้พริกขี้หนู)

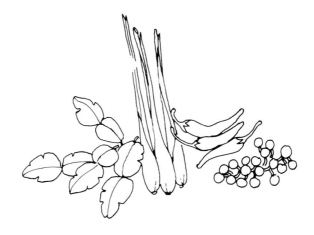

Chicken or Beef Curry

INGREDIENTS FOR SPICE MIXTURE:

1 tbsp. lemon grass	1 tsp. sliced galangal
3 dried chillies	1 tbsp. roasted coriander seeds
5 broiled shallots	1 tsp. roasted cumin seeds
10 broiled garlic cloves	2 tsp. curry powder
1 tsp. broiled ginger	1 tsp. shrimp paste
	1 tsp. salt

OTHER INGREDIENTS:

½ kg chicken or beef	2 tbsp. fried onion
400 grams grated coconut	1 tsp. salt
3 small potatoes, peeled and boiled	

PREPARATION:

- Place spice mixture ingredients in mortar and pound until ground and mixed thoroughly.
- Cut chicken or beef ½ inch thick slices.
- Add 2 cups of water to the coconut and squeeze out 1 cup coconut cream and 2 cups coconut milk. (If making beef curry, squeeze out an additional cup of coconut milk to have enough to cook beef until tender.)
- Fry the spice mixture in 2 tbsp. of the oil used for frying the onions, adding the coconut cream in small amounts. Then add the chicken (or beef) and cook with stirring.
- Spoon into a pot. Add the coconut milk, and if necessary, salt. Cook until the meat is tender, then add the potatoes.
- Remove from heat when done, dip into serving bowl, and sprinkle with fried onion. Serve with Thai pickles or pickled ginger.

THAI PICKLES

INGREDIENTS:

4 cucumbers	1 chilli	2 tsp. sugar
2 shallots	⅓ cup vinegar	1 tsp. salt

PREPARATION:

- Mix the vinegar, sugar, and salt in a pot, bring to a boil, strain, and allow to cool.
- Slice the cucumbers, shallots, and chilli just before serving and add the vinegar mixture.

แกงกะหรี่ไก่ หรือเนื้อ

เครื่องปรุงน้ำพริก

ตะไคร้ซอย	1	ช้อนโต๊ะ	ลูกผักชีคั่ว	1	ช้อนโต๊ะ
พริกแห้ง	3	เม็ด	ยี่หร่าคั่ว	1	ช้อนชา
หอมเผา	5	หัว	ผงกะหรี่	2	ช้อนชา
กระเทียมเผา	10	กลีบ	กะปิ	1	ช้อนชา
ข่าหั่นเล็ก	1	ช้อนชา	เกลือ	1	ช้อนชา

เครื่องปรุงอื่น

เนื้อไก่หรือเนื้อวัว	$\frac{1}{2}$	กิโลกรัม	หอมเจียว	2	ช้อนโต๊ะ
มะพร้าว	400	กรัม	เกลือ	2	ช้อนชา
มันฝรั่งหัวเล็กต้ม	3	หัว			

อาจาด
เครื่องปรุง

แตงกวาหรือแตงร้าน		4	ลูก	น้ำส้มสายชู	$\frac{1}{3}$ ถ้วย
หอมเล็ก		2	หัว	น้ำตาลทราย	2 ช้อนชา
พริกชี้ฟ้าแดง		1	เม็ด	เกลือ	1 ช้อนชา

Two Color Shrimp Balls : ลูกชิ้นกุ้งสองสี

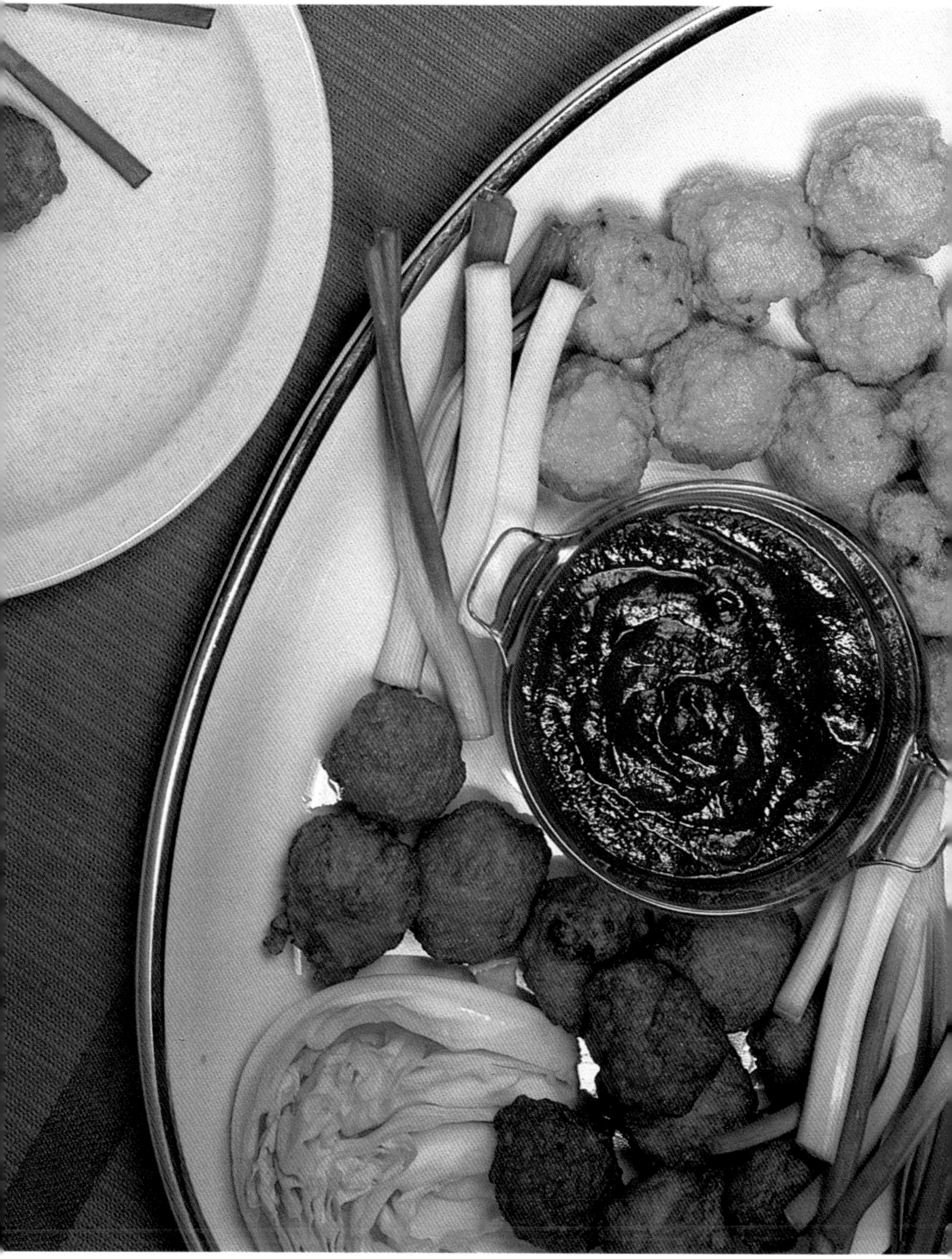

Bean Curd Wrapped in Cabbage *(Kalam Plee Pan Taohoo)*

INGREDIENTS:

8 cabbage leaves	2½ tbsp. sugar
1 tsp. salt	5 tbsp. light soy sauce
8 cocktail toothpicks or 2 celery plants	1 egg
3 cakes soft white bean curd	2 cups chicken soup stock
¼ cup finely chopped garlic plant	1 tbsp. corn flour
300 grams chopped beef	½ lemon, sliced thin

PREPARATION:

- Wash cabbage leaves, taking care not to tear them. Mix salt in water, bring to a boil, and place cabbage leaves in the boiling water until soft. Remove leaves and root from celery and place the stems in the boiling water until soft enough to be used to tie the cabbage leaves closed.
- Fry chopped beef and garlic leaves over low heat, mixing and breaking large lumps. Add ½ tbsp. sugar and 1 tbsp. light soy sauce and cook until the meat is done, then add bean curd and press and turn with spatula to mix with meat. Reduce heat, add beaten egg, and mix in thoroughly.
- Divide mixture into eight portions and dip each onto a cabbage leaf. Fold in ends, then roll up the mixture in the leaf and tie with celery stalk, or pin closed with a toothpick.
- Place the packets in a frying pan, pour in the chicken stock, add the remaining sugar and soy sauce, and simmer over low heat for about 20 minutes.
- Mix the rice flour with 1 tbsp. water and pour into pan, reduce heat, allow the liquid to thicken. Lift the packets onto serving dish and cover with the sauce from the pan, placing the lemon slices on top.

กะหล่ำปลีพันเต้าหู้

เครื่องปรุง

กะหล่ำปลีใบงาม	8	ใบ	น้ำตาล	2½	ช้อนโต๊ะ
เกลือ	1	ช้อนชา	ซีอิ๊วขาว	5	ช้อนโต๊ะ
ไม้จิ้มค็อกเทล	8	อัน	ไข่	1	ฟอง
หรือต้นขึ้นฉ่าย	2	ต้น	น้ำซุปไก่	2	ถ้วย
เต้าหู้ขาวชนิดอ่อน	3	ก้อน	แป้งข้าวโพด	1	ช้อนโต๊ะ
ต้นกระเทียมสับละเอียด	¼	ถ้วย	มะนาวหั่นเป็นแว่นบางๆ ครึ่งลูก		
เนื้อบด	300	กรัม			

Two Color Shrimp Balls *(Luk Chin Kung Song See)*

INGREDIENTS:

½ kg chopped shrimp meat
1 tsp. salt
white of 1 egg
1 tbsp. corn flour

1 tbsp. sherry
1 tsp. cooking oil
¼ tsp. pepper
2 tbsp. tomato catsup
oil for frying shrimp balls

PREPARATION:

- Mix shrimp, salt, egg white, corn flour, sherry, oil, and pepper thoroughly.
- Divide mixture in two and mix the catsup with one portion, giving it a red color. Dip up tablespoons full of the mixture, forming each into a ball.
- Heat oil in deep pan and fry the shrimp balls in hot oil over moderate heat. When done, remove the balls from oil and drain.
- Place on a plate and serve with cucumber, cabbage, sping onion, and a sauce made by mixing catsup with salt and pepper.

ลูกชิ้นกุ้งสองสี

เครื่องปรุง					
กุ้งสับละเอียด	½	กิโลกรัม	น้ำมัน	1	ช้อนชา
เกลือ	1	ช้อนชา	พริกไทย	¼	ช้อนชา
ไข่ขาว	1	ฟอง	แคชชับ	2	ช้อนโต๊ะ
แป้งข้าวโพด	1	ช้อนโต๊ะ	น้ำมันสำหรับทอด		
เหล้าเชอรี่	1	ช้อนโต๊ะ			

Clear Duck Stew : เป็ดตุ๋นน้ำใส

Tom Khlong : ต้มโคล้ง

Clear Duck Stew

INGREDIENTS:
1 fat duck (about 1½ kg)
1 tsp. pepper
1 tsp. salt
2 tsp. dark soy sauce
1 tbsp. Chinese wine
chopped coriander (for garnishing)

SPICE MIXTURE (to be wrapped in cheese cloth)
3 slices mature ginger root about 1 cm thick
15-20 mature coriander roots
15 spring onions
1 one-inch length roasted cinnamon
1 piece cha-em
20 pepper corns, just broken in mortar

PREPARATION:

- Pluck and clean duck, cut into about 12 pieces, and drain. Mix salt, pepper, dark soy sauce, and Chinese wine and brush duck with this mixture. Fry duck in hot oil until golden, remove from pan, blot off oil, and place duck in pot.
- Wrap spice mixture in cheesecloth, tie securely, and place in pot with duck.
- Add water (10-12 cups) and heat strongly until boiling, then reduce to low heat.
- Season with dark and light soy sauces, and simmer until the meat is tender (2-3 hours). Sprinkle with pepper and chopped coriander just before serving and serve with sauce made by mixing 3 tbsp. light soy sauce with 2 tbsp. dark soy sauce.

เป็ดตุ๋นน้ำใส

ส่วนผสม

เป็ดสดตัวอ้วน ๆ ประมาณ	1	ตัว	เกลือป่น	1	ช้อนชา
1½ กิโลกรัม			ซีอิ๊วดำอย่างดี	2	ช้อนชา
พริกไทยป่น	1	ช้อนชา	เหล้าจีน	1	ช้อนโต๊ะ

เครื่องปรุงห่อผ้าขาวบาง

ขิงแก่หั่นหนาประมาณ 1 ซม.	3	ชิ้น	อบเชยเผาไฟยาว 1 นิ้ว	1	ชิ้น
รากผักชีแก่ ๆ	15–20	ราก	ชะเอม	1	ชิ้น
ต้นหอม	15	ต้น	พริกไทยบุบ	20	เม็ด

เครื่องปรุงรส

ซีอิ๊วขาวอย่างดี	3	ช้อนโต๊ะ	ผักชีสำหรับโรยหน้า
ซีอิ๊วดำ	2	ช้อนโต๊ะ	

ใช้น้ำประมาณ 10-12 ถ้วย

Tom Khlong *(Sour Soup)*

INGREDIENTS:

300 grams dried fish (or fresh shrimp)
3 cups water
5-6 shallots
1 tbsp. salt (or 2-3 tbsp. fish sauce)

1 cup young tamarind flowers or leaves (if unavailable, use 2-3 ripe tamarinds)
5 hot chillies (or 1 dried chilli roasted until fragrant)

PREPARATION:

- Wash fish, roast until fragrant, and cut into small slices. Bring water to a boil, then add crushed shallots and fish. Boil until fish is tender, skimming off froth. Add tamarind flowers and season with tamarind (or lemon juice) and salt (or fish sauce) to obtain a sour and salty taste. Add chillies and serve hot.

    If shrimp is used, remove shell and vein, boil a short time, then proceed as above.

ต้มโคล้ง

เครื่องปรุง

ปลาแห้ง หรือปลาช่อนแห้ง	300	กรัม	หอมแดง	5-6 หัว
(หรือใช้กุ้งแทนก็ได้)			เกลือ	1 ช้อนโต๊ะ
น้ำ	3	ถ้วย	(หรือน้ำปลาดี 2-3 ช้อนโต๊ะ	
ใบมะขามอ่อนหรือดอกมะขาม	1	ถ้วย	พริกขี้หนู	5 เม็ด
(ถ้าไม่มีมะขามสด ใช้มะขาม			(หรือใช้พริกแห้งปิ้งไฟให้หอม 1 เม็ด)	
เปียก 2-3 ฝัก)				

Sweet and Sour Fish

INGREDIENTS:

½ kg sea bass (kraphong khao) meat,
sliced into ½ inch thick pieces
2 tbsp. sherry
2 tbsp. light soy sauce
2 tbsp. wheat flour
2 tbsp. corn flour

3 tbsp. cooking oil
Cooking oil for frying fish
1 onion
1 carrot
1 sweet pepper

SAUCE

⅓ cup sugar
¾ cup tomato catsup
¼ cup vinegar
4 tbsp. sherry

½ cup water
1½ tbsp. corn flour
2 pineapple rings, each cut into six
pieces

PREPARATION:

- Marinate the fish in mixture of the sherry, light soy sauce, wheat flour and corn flour.
- Heat oil in deep pan. When hot, fry fish pieces until crisp and golden, then remove and drain.
- Peel onion, slice across, and separate rings. Slice pepper into ½ × 2 inch strips. Peel carrot, cut into 2 × ½ × ¼ inch pieces, and blanch in boiling water.
- Fry onion, pepper, and carrot in 3 tbsp. oil for 1 minute.

SAUCE PREPARATION:

- Mix sugar, catsup, vinegar, and sherry. Mix the flour with the water and stir into the catsup mixture.
- Pour sauce into frying pan and cook over low heat until thickened, then add fish and stir together thoroughly. Dip fish and sauce onto serving dish and surround with pineapple slices.

ปลาเปรี้ยวหวาน

ส่วนผสม

ปลากระพงขาวเอาแต่เนื้อหั่น $\frac{1}{2}$ กิโลกรัม เหล้าเชอรี่ 2 ช้อนโต๊ะ ซีอิ๊วขาว 2 ช้อนโต๊ะ แป้งสาลี 2
ช้อนโต๊ะ แป้งข้าวโพด 2 ช้อนโต๊ะ น้ำมันสำหรับผัด 3 ช้อนโต๊ะ หอมหัวใหญ่ 1 หัว แครอท 1 หัว
พริกหวาน 1 เม็ด

ซอส

น้ำตาล $\frac{1}{3}$ ถ้วย แคชชับ $\frac{1}{3}$ ถ้วย น้ำส้มสายชู $\frac{1}{4}$ ถ้วย เหล้าเชอรี่ 4 ช้อนโต๊ะ น้ำ $\frac{1}{2}$ ถ้วย แป้งข้าวโพด
$1\frac{1}{2}$ ช้อนโต๊ะ สับปะรด 2 แว่น หั่นแว่นละ 6 ชิ้น

Chicken and Wax Gourd Curry *(Kaeng Khua Fuk Kap Kai)*

INGREDIENTS FOR SPICE MIXTURE:

5 dried chillies, seeds removed, soaked in water
1 tsp. salt
1 tsp. minced galangal

1 heaping tbsp. minced lemon grass
10 small shallots
20 garlic cloves
1 tsp. shrimp paste

OTHER INGREDIENTS:

300 grams chicken
400 grams grated coconut
½ kg wax gourd

3 tbsp. tamarind juice
3 tbsp. palm sugar
3 tbsp. fish sauce

PREPARATION:

- Place spice mixture ingredients in a mortar and pound until ground and mixed thoroughly.
- Clean the chicken, cut into 1 inch pieces, mix with 1 tsp. salt, and fry until dry.
- Peel gourd, remove seeds , and cut into 1 inch chunks.
- Add 1½ cups water to coconut and squeeze out 3 cups coconut milk.
- Skim off 1 cup coconut cream, place in frying pan and heat. When oil begins to appear on surface, add the spice mixture and stir in, then add the chicken and cook. Spoon into a pot, add the remaining coconut milk and the wax gourd and heat. When the gourd is done, taste and season with tamarind juice, palm sugar, and fish sauce.

แกงคั่วฟักกับไก่

เครื่องน้ำพริก

พริกแห้ง (แกะเมล็ดออก) แช่			ตะไคร้หั่นละเอียด	1	ช้อนโต๊ะพูน
น้ำ	5	เม็ดเล็ก	หอม	10	หัวเล็ก
เกลือ	1	ช้อนชา	กระเทียม	20	กลีบ
ข่าหั่นละเอียด	1	ช้อนชา	กะปิ	1	ช้อนชา

เครื่องปรุง

เนื้อไก่หั่นชิ้นขนาด 1 นิ้ว	300	กรัม	ส้มมะขามเปียก	3	ช้อนโต๊ะ
มะพร้าว	400	กรัม	น้ำตาลปีบ	3	ช้อนโต๊ะ
ฟักเขียว	$\frac{1}{2}$	กิโลกรัม	น้ำปลา	3	ช้อนโต๊ะ

Beef, Chicken, or Pork Masaman Curry : แกงมัสมั่นเนื้อวัวหรือไก่หรือหมู

Beef, Chicken, or Pork Masaman Curry

INGREDIENTS FOR SPICE MIXTURE:

3 dried chillies, seeds removed, soaked
  in water
1 tsp. salt
1 tsp. minced roasted galangal
1 heaping tbsp. thinly sliced roasted
  lemon grass
5 roasted shallots

2 roasted garlic bulbs
2 cloves, roasted and ground
1 tbsp. ground roasted coriander seeds
1 tsp. ground roasted cumin seeds
5 pepper corns
1 tsp. shrimp paste

OTHER INGREDIENTS:

½ kg beef, chicken, or pork
400 grams grated coconut or 3 cups
  coconut milk
2 tbsp. roasted peanuts
5 peeled small onions (100 grams)
5 small potatoes (100 grams) peeled
  and boiled

3 bay leaves
5 roasted cardamom fruits
1 piece of roasted cinnamon, 1 cm long
3 tbsp. palm sugar
3 tbsp. tamarind juice
3 tbsp. lemon juice

PREPARATION:

- Place spice mixture ingredients in a mortar and pound until ground and mixed thoroughly.
- Cut beef, chicken, or pork into 2 inch chunks.
- Add 1½ cups warm water to the coconut and squeeze out 3 cups coconut milk. Skim off 1 cup coconut cream to be used in cooking spice mixture. Place the remaining coconut milk in a pot with the chicken, pork, or beef and simmer until tender. (If beef is used, 2 additional cups of coconut milk will be needed because of the longer cooking time required.)
- Heat coconut cream in a frying pan until oil appears on surface, then add the spice mixture and cook until fragrant. Spoon into the pot with the meat and add the peanuts. Taste and adjust the flavor so it is sweet, salty, and sour by adding tamarind juice, palm sugar, and lemon juice. Add bay leaves, cardamon, cinnamon, potatoes, and onion and simmer until tender.
- Serve with pickled ginger, pickled cucumbers, or salad.

แกงมัสมั่นเนื้อวัวหรือไก่หรือหมู

เครื่องปรุงน้ำพริก

พริกแห้ง (แกะเมล็ดออก) แช่			กระเทียมเผา	2	หัว
น้ำ	3	เม็ดใหญ่	กานพลูคั่วป่น	2	ดอก
เกลือ	1	ช้อนชา	ลูกผักชีคั่วป่น	1	ช้อนโต๊ะ
ข่าหั่นคั่ว	1	ช้อนชา	ยี่หร่าคั่วป่น	1	ช้อนชา
ตะไคร้หั่นบาง ๆ คั่ว	1 ช้อนโต๊ะพูน		พริกไทย	5	เม็ด
หอมเผา	5	หัว	กะปิ	1	ช้อนชา

เครื่องปรุง

เนื้อวัว หรือไก่ หรือ เนื้อหมู			ลูกกระวานคั่ว	5	ลูก
หั่น 2×2 นิ้ว	$\frac{1}{2}$	กิโลกรัม	อบเชยเผาไฟ ยาวขนาด 1 ซม.	1	อัน
มะพร้าว	400	กรัม	น้ำตาลปีบ	3	ช้อนโต๊ะ
ถั่วลิสงคั่ว	2	ช้อนโต๊ะ	น้ำปลา	3	ช้อนโต๊ะ
หอมฝรั่งหัวเล็ก	5หัว(100กรัม)		น้ำส้มมะขามข้น ๆ	3	ช้อนโต๊ะ
มันฝรั่งหัวเล็กต้มสุกปอกเปลือก	5หัว(100กรัม)		น้ำส้มซ่า	3	ช้อนโต๊ะ
ใบกระวาน	3	ใบ			

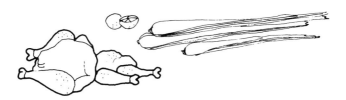

Pork, Chicken, or Fish Hor Mok *(Steamed Curry)*

INGREDIENTS FOR THE SPICE MIXTURE:

5 dried chillies, seeds removed, soaked in water
7 shallots
3 garlic bulbs
2 tbsp. finely sliced galangal
2 tbsp. finely sliced lemon grass

1 tsp. finely sliced kaffir lime rind
2 tsp. finely sliced coriander root
5 pepper corns
1 tsp. salt
1 tsp. shrimp paste
1 tsp. finely sliced kachai (for fish hor mok only)

OHTER INGREDIENTS:

300 grams pork, chicken, or fish
3 tbsp. fish sauce
400 grams grated coconut
1 egg

1 bunch sweet basil (horapha), leaves only
1 coriander plant, root removed
1 chilli
2 kaffir lime leaves

PREPARATION:

- Prepare 15 banana leaf cups 2½ inches in diameter.
- Pound spice mixture until ground and mixed thoroughly.
- If using pork, chop, but not too finely. If chicken, cut into small pieces. If fish, cut into thin slices. If featherback fish is used, scrape flesh from fish and knead in 1 tbsp. finely ground coriander root and pepper. Marinate whichever meat with 1 tbsp. fish sauce.
- Mix ½ cup water with coconut, then squeeze out 1½ cups coconut milk. Squeeze again to obtain another ½ cup coconut milk, and then a third time to get another ½ cup of milk.
- Mix ¾ cup coconut cream from the first squeezing with 1 tsp. rice flour, heat to boiling, remove from heat, and set aside to be used to top the hor mok.
- Mix the remaining coconut milk from the first squeezing with the spice mixture, then stir in the meat, next the egg, the fish sauce, and then the rest of the coconut milk a little at a time. Finally stir in a little each of sweet basil, coriander, and kaffir lime leaves to add fragrance.
- Line the bottoms of the banana leaf cups with the remaining sweet basil leaves, fill each cup with the meat mixture, and steam for 14 minutes. Then remove steamer trays, pour some coconut cream onto each hor mok, sprinkle each with coriander, kaffir lime leaves, and chilli, steam for another minute, then remove from steamer.

In place of sweet basil leaves, yaw leaves, cabbage, or bamboo shoots cut up and steamed may be used to line the banana leaf cups. Pre-steaming minimizes subsidence of hor mok in the cups.

ห่อหมกหมู หรือไก่ หรือปลา

เครื่องปรุงน้ำพริก

พริกแห้ง (แกะเมล็ดออก)	5	เม็ด	ผิวมะกรูดหั่นละเอียด	1	ช้อนชา
แช่น้ำ			รากผักชีหั่นละเอียด	2	ช้อนชา
หอม	7	หัว	พริกไทย	5	เม็ด
กระเทียม	3	หัว	เกลือ	1	ช้อนชา
ข่าหั่นละเอียด	2	ช้อนโต๊ะ	กะปิ	1	ช้อนชา
ตะไคร้หั่นละเอียด	2	ช้อนโต๊ะ	ถ้าใช้ปลา ใส่กระชาย	1	ช้อนชา

เครื่องปรุงอื่น

เนื้อหมู หรือไก่หรือปลา	300	กรัม	ใบโหระพาเด็ดใบ	1	กำ
น้ำปลา	3	ช้อนโต๊ะ	ผักชี	1	ต้น
มะพร้าว	400	กรัม	พริกแดง	1	เม็ด
ไข่	1	ฟอง	ใบมะกรูด	2	ใบ

Tom Chab Chai *(Chinese Vegetable Soup)*

INGREDIENTS:

200 grams belly of pork, sliced into ½-¾ inch cubes

Half of a chicken or duck, cut into 1½ inch chunks

3-4 cups white radish (2 medium size young white radish peeled and cut into 1 inch long pieces, each of which is quartered)

1 head Chinese cabbage, cut into short sections

1 head cabbage, washed, quartered, cored, and cut into 1 inch cubes

1 cup leek plant, cut into 1 in long pieces

2 cups celery, washed and cut into short pieces

3-4 cups sliced kale, stems crushed

5-10 medium size dried Chinese mushrooms, soaked in water, stalks removed

5 hard yellow soybean curd cakes, cut into quarters, each quarter sliced diagonally

3 cups mung bean noodles, soaked, cut into short lengths, and drained

5-6 tbsp. soybean paste

2 tbsp. chopped garlic

2-3 tbsp. fish sauce or light soy sauce

2 tbsp. dark soy sauce

2 tbsp. palm sugar

4 tbsp. cooking oil

7-8 cups of water

PREPARATION:

- Bring water to a boil then add the belly of pork, the duck or chicken, the fish sauce or light soy sauce, and the dark soy sauce. Boil uncovered until the meats are done, skimming off froth that forms.
- When the meats are done, add all the vegetables, the bean curd, and the mung bean noodles.
- Heat oil in frying pan and brown the garlic, then add the soybean paste and fry until fragrant.
- Add the fried garlic and soybean paste and the sugar to the soup. Taste and add fish sauce if necessary.
- Simmer until the vegetables are well done.

The soup may be kept for a few days but must be reheated each day. The ingredients may be altered; the important items are the pork belly and three or four kinds of leafy vegetables.

ต้มจับฉ่าย

เครื่องปรุง

หมูสามชั้นเนื้อหนาหนังบาง 200 กรัม เป็ดสด 1 ซีก หรือไก่ด้วยก็ได้ หัวผักกาดขาวอ่อน ขนาดกลาง 2 หัว คะน้ำทุบก้านตัดเป็นท่อน ๆ 3-4 ถ้วย ผักกาดขาวตัดท่อนเท่าผักคะน้ำ 1 ต้น ต้นกระเทียมตัดท่อน ๆ 1 ถ้วย ขึ้นฉ่ายทั้งต้นและใบ 2 ถ้วย กะหล่ำปลี 1 หัว เห็ดหอมขนาด กลางประมาณ 5-10 ดอก เต้าหู้เหลืองชนิดแข็ง 5 แผ่น วุ้นเส้นแช่น้ำ ตัดให้สั้น ๆ 3 ถ้วย เต้าเจี้ยวน้ำ (อย่างดี) หอม ๆ 5-6 ช้อนโต๊ะ กระเทียมสับ 2 ช้อนโต๊ะ น้ำปลาหรือซีอิ๊วขาว 2-3 ช้อนโต๊ะ ซีอิ๊วดำหวาน 2 ช้อนชา น้ำตาลปีบ 2 ช้อนโต๊ะ น้ำมัน 4 ช้อนโต๊ะ น้ำ 7-8 ถ้วย

Kaeng Liang *(Vegetable Soup Thai Style)*

INGREDIENTS FOR SPICE MIXTURE:

10 pepper corns

1 tbsp. shrimp paste

2-3 tbsp. fish sauce

10 shallots

½ cup dried shrimp or fish

OTHER INGREDIENTS:

5 cups (½ kg) of one of the following: sponge gourd, bottle-gourd, gord gourd, phak wan, or banana flower

5 stems of sweet basil (maenglak)

4 cups soup stock or water

PREPARATION:

- Place spice mixture ingredients in a mortar and pound until mixed thoroughly.
- Add spice mixture to soup stock (or water) in a pot and heat to boiling, stirring to prevent sticking. Do not cover the pot or allow to boil over.
- Wash the vegetables. If gourd is used, peel and cut into 1½ inch strips. Other vegetables are separated into individual leaves or bracts.
- When the water boils, add fish sauce, or, if this odor is offensive, salt may be substituted. Add vegetables and boil. When vegetables are done, taste and add fish sauce or salt as desired, then remove from heat.

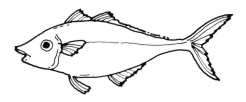

แกงเลียง

เครื่องน้ำพริก

พริกไทย	10	เม็ด	กุ้งแห้งหรือปลากรอบ	$\frac{1}{2}$ ถ้วย
หัวหอม	10	หัว	น้ำซุป	4 ถ้วย
กะปิ	1	ช้อนโต๊ะ	น้ำปลาดี	2-3 ช้อนโต๊ะ

ผักที่ใช้แกง

บวบเหลี่ยม น้ำเต้า ผักตำลึง ผักหวาน หัวปลี ฯลฯอย่างใดอย่างหนึ่ง 5 ถ้วย ($\frac{1}{2}$ กิโลกรัม) ใบแมงลัก 5 กิ่ง

Kaeng Choed Ruam Mit *(Ruam Mit Soup)*

INGREDIENTS:

½ cup chicken
½ cup pork
2 chicken livers
2 chicken gizzards
½ cup shelled shrimp

1 white radish
1 carrot
¼ tsp. pepper
5 cups soup stock
1-2 tbsp. light soy sauce or fish sauce
coriander and spring onions

PREPARATION:

• Slice chicken and pork into small pieces. Make several slits in the gizzards to open them up. Cut the livers into thin slices.

• Wash and peel the radish and carrot, cut channels down the length, then cut into ¼ inch thick slices (or carve to look like flowers or leaves)

• Heat soup stock, add radish and carrot, and cook over low heat until tender, then add the pork, chicken, shrimp, liver, and gizzards, boil and season to taste. When done, add a little sliced spring onion. Dip into serving bowl, sprinkle with pepper and coriander, and serve immediately.

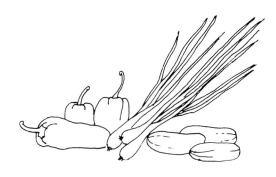

เครื่องปรุง			แกงจืดรวมมิตร		
เนื้อไก่เนื้อหมูอย่างละ ½ ถ้วย	200	กรัม	แครอท	1	หัว
เครื่องในไก่	2	พวง	พริกไทยป่น	¼	ช้อนชา
กุ้งชีแฮ้แกะเปลือกแล้ว	½	ถ้วย	น้ำซุป	5	ถ้วย
(กุ้งปอกเปลือก 200 กรัม)			ซีอิ๊วขาวหรือน้ำปลาดี	1-2	ช้อนโต๊ะ
หัวผักกาดขาว	1	หัว	ผักชี ต้นหอม		

Chicken with Galangal Shoots in Coconut Milk

INGREDIENTS:

6 chicken drumsticks
½ cup thin slices of young galangal
(cut across)
½ kg grated coconut
1 lemon grass stem

3-4 kaffir lime leaves
3 tbsp. fish sauce
3 lemons
10 hot chillies
1 coriander plant, root removed

PREPARATION:

- Wash drumsticks thoroughly, having removed any feathers.
- Mix 2 cups water with coconut, then squeeze out 3 cups coconut milk. Skim off ½ cup coconut cream and set aside. Heat the remaining coconut milk to boiling, then add the galangal, the lemon grass cut into sections and crushed, the kaffir lime leaves, drumsticks, and fish sauce, and simmer over low heat. When the chicken has become tender, add the coconut cream, stir and, when the liquid again boils, remove from heat.
- Season with fish sauce, lemon juice, and crushed hot chillies, dip into serving dish, and sprinkle with coriander.

ต้มข่าน่องไก่กะทิสด

เครื่องปรุง				
น่องไก่	6	น่อง	น้ำปลา	3	ช้อนโต๊ะ
ข่าอ่อนหั่นขวางบาง ๆ	$\frac{1}{2}$ ถ้วย		มะนาว	3	ผล
มะพร้าวขูด	$\frac{1}{2}$	กิโลกรัม	พริกขี้หนู	10	เม็ด
ตะไคร้	1	ต้น	ผักชี	1	ต้น
ใบมะกรูด	3-4	ใบ			

Sour Fish Soup with Swamp Cabbage and Fresh Chillies *(Kaeng Som Phak Bung Phrik Sod Kab Pla)*

INGREDIENTS FOR CHILLI PASTE:

3 chillies	5 cloves garlic	1 tsp. shrimp paste
7 shallots	1 tsp. salt	

OTHER INGREDIENTS:

½ kg fish	10 tomatoes, sliced	3-4 tbsp. fish sauce
1 kg swamp cabbage	2-3 tbsp. lemon juice	

PREPARATION:

- Place chilli paste ingredients in mortar and pound until ground and mixed thoroughly.
- Wash the fish and cut into ½ inch thick slices.
- Select young swamp cabbage stems and cut into short pieces.
- Place 2 cups water in a pot and heat. When the water boils, stir in the chilli paste and then add the swamp cabbage. When this is cooked, taste and add fish sauce and lemon juice so the flavor is sour and salty. Add the tomato, and when the soup boils again, add the fish and cover. When the fish is done, remove from heat.

แกงส้มผักบุ้งพริกสดกับปลา

เครื่องปรุงน้ำพริก

พริกชี้ฟ้าสด	3	เม็ด	เกลือ	1	ช้อนชา
หอม	7	หัว	กะปิ	1	ช้อนชา
กระเทียม	5	กลีบ			

เครื่องปรุงอื่น

ปลาขอดเกล็ดเอาไส้ออก	$\frac{1}{2}$	กิโลกรัม	น้ำมะนาว	2-3	ช้อนโต๊ะ
ผักบุ้งก้านอ่อนหั่นท่อนสั้น ๆ	1	กิโลกรัม	น้ำปลา	3-4	ช้อนโต๊ะ
มะเขือเทศผ่าซีก	10	ผลเล็ก			

Fresh Mushroom Tom Yam

(Sour Soup with Fresh Mushrooms)

INGREDIENTS:

1 kg fresh mushrooms
2 lemon grass stalks
5 kaffir lime leaves
2 coriander plants, roots removed
10 hot chillies

1-2 dried chillies
3-4 lemons
½ kg grated coconut
2-3 tbsp. fish sauce

PREPARATION:

- Wash mushrooms; if large, cut in half or in thirds.
- Wash lemon grass, slice, and crush. Tear kaffir lime leaves.
- Wash coriander and chop up coarsely.
- Just break hot chillies in a mortar. Roast dried chillies, then break into pieces.
- Mix 2 cups water with coconut, then squeeze out 3 cups coconut milk, and heat. When boiling, add lemon grass, kaffir lime leaves, and mushrooms, and and season with fish sauce. When the mushrooms are done, remove from heat, and add lemon juice, hot chillies, and dried chillies. Dip into serving bowl and sprinkle with chopped coriander.

ต้มยำเห็ดสด

เครื่องปรุง					
เห็ดสด	1	กิโลกรัม	พริกแห้ง	1–2	เม็ด
ตะไคร้	2	ต้น	มะนาว	3–4	ผล
ใบมะกรูด	5	ใบ	มะพร้าว	$\frac{1}{2}$	กิโลกรัม
ผักชี	2	ต้น	น้ำปลา	2–3	ช้อนโต๊ะ
พริกขี้หนู	10	เม็ด			

Sweet and Salty Fresh Mackerel Stew

INGREDIENTS:

20 fresh mackerel
1 tsp. sliced coriander root
7 pepper corns
1 tbsp. crushed garlic
3 tbsp. salt

½ cup palm sugar
4 tbsp. dark soy sauce
4 tbsp. cooking oil
3 ripe tamarinds
1 ten-inch length sugar cane

PREPARATION:

- Wash mackerel, remove gills and intestines, slit off bony gill covers on both sides, cut off the head and tail, wash to remove all slime, and place the cut head in the belly of the fish.
- Peel sugar cane, split lengthwise into several pieces, and cut as long as the diameter of the pot. Flatten and line the bottom of the pot with sugar cane, then arrange the fish in layers on the cane. Cover fish with water and add salt, dark soy sauce, palm sugar, and tamarind. Heat strongly to boiling, then reduce heat and simmer.
- Pound coriander root, pepper, and garlic until ground and mixed thoroughly, fry in the oil until fragrant, and add to the pot. Taste and season to obtain a sweet and salty taste and continue simmering until the liquid permeates the fish flesh. Can be kept for several days. When serving, add sliced onion, chilli, and lemon juice.

Red snapper, climbing perch, or serpent head fish can also be used.

ต้มเค็มปลาทูสด

เครื่องปรุง					
ปลาทูสดตัวงาม ๆ	20	ตัว	น้ำตาลปีบ	$\frac{1}{2}$	ถ้วย
รากผักชีหั่นแล้ว	1	ช้อนชา	ซีอิ๊วดำ	4	ช้อนโต๊ะ
พริกไทย	7	เมล็ด	น้ำมันพืช	3	ช้อนโต๊ะ
กระเทียม	1	ช้อนโต๊ะ	ส้มมะขามเปียก	3	ฝัก
เกลือ	3	ช้อนโต๊ะ	อ้อย (ยาว 10 นิ้ว)	1	ท่อน

Sour Fresh Mackerel Soup

INGREDIENTS:

5 fresh mackerel
1 tbsp. sliced coriander root
7 pepper corns
5 shallots
1 tsp. shrimp paste
¼ cup tamarind juice

1 tbsp. shredded young ginger, washed
  in salt water
5 tbsp. palm sugar
3 tbsp. fish sauce
5 spring onions, cut into 1 inch lengths
3 coriander plants
3 cups water

PREPARATION:

- Wash mackerel, gut , remove head and tail, and wash all slime off.
- Pound together coriander root, pepper, shallots, and shrimp paste until well blended, mix with 3 cups water in a pot, and heat. Add tamarind juice, palm sugar, and fish sauce. When boiling, add mackerel and shredded ginger.
- When fish are done, add spring onion, stir, and remove from heat. Dip into serving bowl, sprinkle with chopped coriander, and serve hot.

Other fish, such as serpenthead and climbing perch, as well as chicken may be used.

ต้มส้มปลาทูสด

เครื่องปรุง					
ปลาทูสดตัวงาม ๆ	5	ตัว	น้ำส้มมะขามเปียกข้น ๆ	$\frac{1}{4}$	ถ้วย
รากผักชีหั่น	1	ช้อนโต๊ะ	น้ำตาลปีบ	5	ช้อนโต๊ะ
พริกไทย	7	เมล็ด	น้ำปลา	3	ช้อนโต๊ะ
หอมแดง	5	หัว	ต้นหอมตัดยาว 1 นิ้ว	5	ต้น
กะปิ	1	ช้อนชา	ผักชี	3	ต้น
ขิงซอย (ล้างน้ำเกลือ)	1	ช้อนโต๊ะ			

Khao Man : ข้าวมัน

Som Tam Malakor : ส้มตำมะละกอ

Neua Khem Phad Wan : เนื้อเค็มผัดหวาน

Som Tam Malakor *(Papaya Salad)*

INGREDIENTS:

1 peeled and shredded green papaya
(about 4 cups)
6 garlic cloves
1 dried chilli soaked in water
7 pepper corns
1 tbsp. tamarind juice
3 tbsp. fish sauce

3 tbsp. palm sugar
2 tbsp. lemon juice
¼ cup ground dried shrimp
¼ cup lemon cut into small cubes
Cabbage, lettuce and leaves of chaphu
and coral tree

PREPARATION:

- Gently crush shredded papaya in mortar with pestle. Remove and set aside.
- Crush garlic, dried chilli, and pepper corns in mortar, mixing thoroughly.
- Mix tamarind juice, fish sauce, and sugar in a pot and heat to a boil. Remove from heat, allow to cool, add lemon juice, and mix with chilli paste in mortar.
- Add the crushed papaya, the dried shrimp, and the lemon cubes and mix thoroughly.
- Serve with lettuce and other vegetables.

ส้มตำมะละกอ

เครื่องปรุง						
มะละกอดิบ 1 ผล ขูดหรือสับ	4–5	ถ้วย	น้ำปลา		3	ช้อนโต๊ะ
เส้นเล็ก ๆ			น้ำตาลปีบ		3	ช้อนโต๊ะ
กระเทียม	6	กลีบ	น้ำมะนาว		2	ช้อนโต๊ะ
พริกแห้งแช่น้ำ	1	เม็ด	กุ้งแห้งป่น		$\frac{1}{4}$	ถ้วย
พริกไทย	7	เม็ด	มะนาวหั่นสี่เหลี่ยมเล็ก ๆ		$\frac{1}{4}$	ถ้วย
น้ำส้มมะขาม	1	ช้อนโต๊ะ	ผักกาดหอม ใบชะพลู ใบทองหลาง			

Neua Khem Phad Wan *(Sweet Fried Dried Beef)*

INGREDIENTS:

200 grams dried salted beef
¼ cup fried, thinly sliced shallots

¼ cup cooking oil
¼ cup sugar

PREPARATION:

- Wash beef, steam 15 minutes, pound to soften, and then tear into very thin strips. Fry beef in the oil over low heat until crisp, adding more oil if necessary. When crisp, add the sugar and half of the fried shallots. Sprinkle the other half over the beef before serving.

เนื้อเค็มผัดหวาน

เครื่องปรุง

เนื้อเค็ม	200 กรัม	น้ำมัน	$\frac{1}{4}$	ถ้วย
หอมเจียว	$\frac{1}{4}$ ถ้วย	น้ำตาลทราย	$\frac{1}{4}$	ถ้วย

Khao Man Som Tam *(Rice Cooked in Coconut Milk and Eaten with Papaya Salad)*

INGREDIENTS:

1½ cups (300 grams) rice
300 grams grated coconut

2 tbsp. sugar
2 tsp. salt

PREPARATION:

- Wash the rice once and place in a colander to drain.
- Add 2½ cups water to the coconut and squeeze out 3 cups coconut milk. Add the sugar and salt and stir until dissolved. Strain into a pot and add the rice. Boil or steam until the rice is done (about 30 minutes).

ข้าวมัน–ส้มตำ

เครื่องปรุง

ข้าวสารงาม ๆ (300 กรัม)	$1\frac{1}{2}$ ถ้วย	น้ำตาลทราย	2	ช้อนโต๊ะ
มะพร้าว	300 กรัม	เกลือ	2	ช้อนชา

Khao Moo Daeng : ข้าวหมูแดง

Khao Moo Daeng *(Rice with Red Pork)*

INGREDIENTS:

½ kg pock loin
¼ cup tomato paste
1½ cups water
4 tbsp. light soy sauce

4 tbsp. sugar
2 tbsp. dark soy sauce
2 tbsp. vinegar

cucumbers, sliced ¼
inch thick
coriander leaves
chillies, sliced into thin
rings

PREPARATION:

- Cut pork into long strips 2 in. thick. With a fork, work the pork strips around in a marinade made of the tomato paste, light soy sauce, and 2 tbsp. sugar. Let stand a short while then place in a pot, add water, heat to a boil, reduce heat, and simmer. When the pork is tender, remove from pot and roast over low heat or in an oven until browned all over. Allow pork to cool, then cut into thin slices.
- For gravy, season 1 cup of the juices in the pot the pork was cooked in, then heat and thicken with 1 tbsp. flour mixed with 2 tbsp. water. When thickened, remove from heat.
- Arrange pork and cucumber attractively on plates of rice, spoon gravy over the pork, and garnish with coriander leaves.
- Serve with sauce made by dissolving remaining sugar in the dark soy sauce and vinegar and adding sliced chillies.

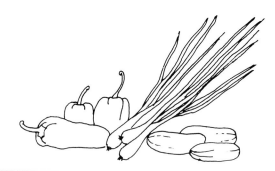

ข้าวหมูแดง

เครื่องปรุง					
หมูสันนอก	$\frac{1}{2}$	กิโลกรัม	ซีอิ๊วดำ	2	ช้อนโต๊ะ
ซอสมะเขือเทศ	$\frac{1}{4}$	ถ้วย	น้ำส้ม	2	ช้อนโต๊ะ
น้ำประมาณ	$1\frac{1}{2}$	ถ้วย	แตงกวาหั่นเป็นชิ้นหนา $\frac{1}{4}$ นิ้ว	5	ลูก
ซีอิ๊วขาว	4	ช้อนโต๊ะ	ผักชีเด็ดเป็นใบ ๆ พริกแดงหั่น		
น้ำตาลทราย	4	ช้อนโต๊ะ	เป็นแว่นบาง ๆ		

Khao Kha Moo *(Fresh Ham on Rice)*

INGREDIENTS:

2½-3 shank portion of fresh ham
5-6 coriander roots
4-5 cloves garlic, crushed flat
10 pepper corns

2 tbsp. anise seed powder (or 2 tbsp.
  ground cinnamon instead)
¼ cup light soy sauce
2 tbsp. dark soy sauce
300 grams pickled Chinese cabbage

PREPARATION:

- Wash fresh ham, having removed any hair by scorching in an open flame and then scraping.
- Place ham in a pot and cover with water. Add coriander roots, garlic, pepper, anise seed powder and light and dark soy sauces. Cover pot, bring to a boil, then reduce heat, and cook until ham becomes tender.
- Serve with rice, boiled pickled cabbage, and sauce made by mixing 2 well-pounded chillies with ¼ cup vinegar and 3 tbsp. dark soy sauce and which is placed in a small dish.

ข้าวขาหมู

เครื่องปรุง				
ขาหมู	$2\frac{1}{2}$ –3 กก.	ซีอิ๊วดำ	2	ช้อนโต๊ะ
รากผักชี	5–6 ราก	ใบผักกาดดอง	300	กรัม
กระเทียม (ทุบให้แบน)	4–5 กลีบ	พริกชี้ฟ้าหรือพริกเหลือง	2	เม็ด
พริกไทยเม็ด	10 เม็ด	น้ำส้ม	$\frac{1}{4}$	ถ้วย
ผงพะโล้	2 ช้อนโต๊ะ	ซีอิ๊วดำ	3	ช้อนโต๊ะ
ซีอิ๊วขาว	$\frac{1}{4}$ ถ้วย			

Khao Rad Na Kai : ข้าวราดหน้าไก่

Khao Rad Na Kai *(Chicken in Sauce on Rice)*

INGREDIENTS:

350 grams rice
300 grams chicken
100 grams chicken livers
1 onion
100 grams mushrooms, halved
100 grams Chinese mustard green
  (Phak Kwangtung)
1 cup (100 grams) spring onions cut
  into 1 inch lengths
2 coriander plants, root removed

3 tbsp. light soy sauce
2½ cup chicken stock
3 tbsp. tapioca flour mixed in ¼ cup
  water
1 tsp. sugar
1 tbsp. chopped garlic
2 tbsp. cooking oil
½ tsp. pepper
3 chillies
¼ cup vinegar

PREPARATION:

- Wash the rice, divide into five portions and place each in a steaming cup. Add 2/3 cup water to each cup and steam until done.
- Cut chicken meat and livers into small pieces and marinate in 1 tbsp. light soy sauce.
- Peel and wash onion, cut in half, then cut across into thin slices.
- Heat oil in frying pan, brown the garlic, then add chicken meat and livers and fry until done. Add the onion slices. When cooked, add the mushrooms, mustard green, and hot chicken stock. Add light soy sauce and sugar to taste and thicken with the tapioca flour in water. When boiling, taste and season as necessary, then add the spring onion and remove from heat.
- Invert cups of rice on serving plates and tap to remove rice. Dip the hot chicken and sauce over the rice, sprinkle with chopped coriander and pepper, and serve immediately.
- Serve with the chilli cut into thin rings in vinegar.

ข้าวราดหน้าไก่

เครื่องปรุง

ข้าวสาร	350	กรัม	น้ำสต๊อก	$2\frac{1}{2}$	ถ้วย
เนื้อไก่	300	กรัม	แป้งมัน 3 ช้อนโต๊ะละลายน้ำ	$\frac{1}{4}$	ถ้วย
ตับไก่	100	กรัม	น้ำตาลทราย	1	ช้อนชา
หอมใหญ่	1	หัว	กระเทียมสับ	1	ช้อนโต๊ะ
เห็ดบัวผ่าครึ่ง	100	กรัม	น้ำมัน	2	ช้อนโต๊ะ
ผักกวางตุ้งตัดท่อนสั้น 1 นิ้ว	100	กรัม	พริกไทยป่น	$\frac{1}{2}$	ช้อนชา
ต้นหอมตัดเป็นท่อน	3	ต้น	พริกแดง	3	เม็ด
ผักชี	2	ต้น	น้ำส้ม	$\frac{1}{4}$	ถ้วย
ซีอิ๊วขาว	3	ช้อนโต๊ะ			

Khao Man Kai *(Chicken with Rice Cooked in Chicken Broth)*

INGREDIENTS:

2 chicken breasts or thighs (300 grams)
3 cups water
1 tsp. salt
2 crushed coriander roots
1½ cups rice

3 tbsp. cooking oil
10 slightly crushed garlic cloves
5 cucumbers
1 coriander plant, root removed

PREPARATION:

- Place chicken in pot with 3 cups water, salt, and coriander roots and boil until chicken is done. Skim off froth, and use low heat to get a clear broth. Remove chicken from pot, bone it, and cut into thin slices. Strain the broth.
- Wash rice, pour off water, and allow to stand a while.
- Heat oil in frying pan and add garlic. Before garlic browns, add rice and fry 3 minutes. Dip rice into a pot, add 2½ cups chicken broth, and cook until rice is done.
- Spoon rice onto plates, arrange chicken slices on top and garnish with coriander. Slice cucumber into ¼ inch rings and put on side of plates. Serve with fermented soybean sauce.

FERMENTED SOYBEAN SAUCE INGREDIENTS:

3 tbsp. fermented soy beans
1 tsp. dark soy sauce
1 tbsp. vinegar

1 tsp. sugar
1 tbsp. mature ginger, well pounded
1 chilli, well pounded

PREPARATION:

Strain fermented soy beans and collect the liquid. Pound the solid portion thoroughly and mix with the liquid. Mix in the soy sauce, vinegar, sugar, ginger, and chilli. Spoon into small dish.

ข้าวมันไก่

เครื่องปรุง

ไก่อกหรือขา (300 กรัม)	2	ชิ้น	น้ำมัน	3	ช้อนโต๊ะ
น้ำสำหรับต้มไก่	3	ถ้วย	กระเทียมทุบพอแตก	10	กลีบ
เกลือ	1	ช้อนชา	แตงกวา	5	ผล
รากผักชีทุบ	2	ราก	ผักชี	1	ต้น
ข้าวสาร (250 กรัม)	1½	ถ้วย			

น้ำเต้าเจี้ยว

เต้าเจี้ยวดำ	3	ช้อนโต๊ะ	น้ำตาลทราย	1	ช้อนชา
ซีอิ๊วดำ	1	ช้อนชา	ขิงแก่โขลกละเอียด	1	เม็ด
น้ำส้ม	1	ช้อนโต๊ะ	พริกแดงโขลกละเอียด	1	เม็ด

Khao Phad See Muang

INGREDIENTS:

1½ cups (300 grams) rice
150 grams pork, sliced into small pieces
1½ tbsp. shrimp paste mixed with 1 tbsp. water
1 tbsp. fish sauce
4 shallots, chopped
¼ cup chopped or pounded dried shrimp

1 tbsp. finely chopped garlic
2 lemons
6 madan, shredded
1 tsp. sugar
¼ cup cooking oil
1 egg
1 coriander plant
1 finely sliced chilli
6 cucumbers

PREPARATION:

- Steam rice, using 2½ cups water, about 40 minutes, then rake to separate grains.
- Fry garlic until golden then add pork and fry. Add shrimp paste; when fragrant, add sugar, fish sauce, and shrimp and fry, mixing together.
- Add rice and continue frying. When done, remove from heat, sprinkle with madan and shallots, mix together thoroughly, and remove from pan.
- Beat the egg. Heat 1 tsp. oil in pan, pour in egg and swirl so egg forms thin layer on bottom of pan. When egg sets, roll up and cut into narrow strips.
- Scoop rice onto plate and sprinkle with egg, coriander, and chilli. Serve with sliced cucumber and lemon.

ข้าวผัดสีม่วง

เครื่องปรุง					
ข้าวสาร (1½ ถ้วย)	300	กรัม	มะดันซอย	6	ผล
เนื้อหมูหั่นเล็ก ๆ	150	กรัม	น้ำตาลทราย	1	ช้อนชา
กะปิดี 1½ ช้อนโต๊ะละลายน้ำ	1	ช้อนโต๊ะ	น้ำมัน	¼	ถ้วย
น้ำปลา	1	ช้อนโต๊ะ	ไข่	1	ฟอง
หอมซอย	4	หัว	ผักชี	1	ต้น
กระเทียมสับละเอียด	1	ช้อนโต๊ะ	พริกแดงหั่นฝอย	1	เม็ด
กุ้งแห้งหั่นเล็ก ๆ หรือป่นแล้ว	¼	ถ้วย	แตงกวา	6	ผล
มะนาว	2	ผล			

Fried Rice with Fermented Curd Cake

INGREDIENTS:

4 cups cooked rice	10 madan
2 fermented bean curd cakes	1 egg
300 grams pork	5 cucumbers
2 tbsp. cooking oil	1 spring onion
2 tbsp. palm sugar	1 coriander plant
1 tbsp. fish sauce	1 hot chillies

PREPARATION:

- Mix rice with curd cake.
- Slice pork into small, thin pieces, fry in 1 tbsp. oil, add sugar, fish sauce, and half of the chopped shallot. Continue frying until dry.
- Add rice, mix thoroughly with pork, fry until done, then remove from pan.
- Heat a little oil in pan, pour in beaten egg, swirl to spread egg thinly over bottom of pan, then roll up and cut into shreds for sprinkling on rice.
- Scoop rice onto plate, sprinkle with madan, egg, coriander, and spring onion. Place ¼ inch thick cucumber slices and chilli on side of plate.

ข้าวผัดเต้าหู้ยี้

เครื่องปรุง					
ข้าวสุก	4	ถ้วย	หอมซอย	10	หัว
เต้าหู้ยี้	2	แผ่น	มะดันซอย (หรือมะนาว)	10	ผล
เนื้อหมู	300	กรัม	ไข่เป็ด	1	ฟอง
น้ำมัน	2	ช้อนโต๊ะ	แตงกวา	5	ผล
น้ำตาลปีบ	2	ช้อนโต๊ะ	ต้นหอม ผักชี อย่างละ	2	ต้น
น้ำปลา	1	ช้อนโต๊ะ	พริกขี้หนู	10	เม็ด

Fried Rice with Fermented Pork

INGREDIENTS:

6 cups cooked rice, raked to separate grains

1 cup sliced fermented pork (slice 1 large or 4 small packets diagonally)

2 onions, sliced top to bottom not too thinly

2 tbsp. chopped crushed garlic cloves

5-6 eggs

2 tbsp. fish sauce

1 tbsp. sugar

1 tsp. pepper

cucumbers, spring onions, and coriander

lemon (if desired)

PREPARATION:

• Heat oil in frying pan. Fry garlic until fragrant, then add onions and fermented pork and fry until done. Beat eggs, pour over pork and fry until done, turning regularly. Then add the rice, mix in, and fry. Add fish sauce, sugar, and pepper and mix thoroughly. When done, dip onto plates and garnish with chopped coriander. Place spring onions and sliced cucumber on sides of plates.

ข้าวผัดแหนม

เครื่องปรุง

ข้าวสวยซุยให้กระจาย	6	ถ้วย	ไข่เป็ด หรือ ไข่ไก่	5-6 ฟอง
แหนมหมูหั่นแฉลบ (ห่อใหญ่			น้ำปลา	2 ช้อนโต๊ะ
1 ห่อ หรือ ห่อเล็ก 4 ห่อ)	1	ถ้วย	น้ำตาล	1 ช้อนโต๊ะ
หอมใหญ่ หั่นตามยาวของหัว			พริกไทยป่น	1 ช้อนชา
ไม่บางมาก	2	หัว	แตงกวา ต้นหอม ผักชี มะนาว	
กระเทียมทุบสับละเอียด	2	ช้อนโต๊ะ	(ถ้าไม่เปรี้ยว)	

Fried Rice with Pork and Egg

INGREDIENTS:

300 grams (1½ cups) rice (not re-
  cently harvested)
2½ cups water
150 grams pork
2 eggs
¼ cup cooking oil
100 grams onion
2 tbsp. tomato catsup

1 tbsp. sugar
3 tbsp. light soy sauce
1 coriander plant, root removed
1 chilli
6 cucumbers
6 spring onions
2 limes or lemons

PREPARATION:

- Steam rice in 2½ cups water until done (about 40 minutes) and then stir to separate grains.
- Cut pork into thin slices and marinate in 1 tbsp. light soy sauce for a short time.
- Slice onion into ½ cm thick rings.
- Fry onion in oil. When done, add the pork, catsup, sugar, and soy sauce and stir together. Then add the rice and fry. When done, remove from pan.
- Fry eggs in 1 tbsp. oil, turning and breaking regularly. When done, mix in the rice and season to taste.
- Cut cucumbers into ¼ inch thick rings and slice chillies into long shreds.
- Dip rice onto plates and garnish with chopped coriander and the chillies, Serve with cucumber slices, spring onions, and lemon wedges on side of plate.

ข้าวผัดหมูใส่ไข่

เครื่องปรุง

ข้าวสาร(ข้าวเก่า)	300	กรัม	น้ำตาลทราย	1	ช้อนโต๊ะ
	(1½ ถ้วย)		ซีอิ๊วขาว	3	ช้อนโต๊ะ
เนื้อหมูหั่นชิ้นเล็ก ๆ	150	กรัม	ผักชี	1	ต้น
ไข่ไก่	2	ฟอง	พริกแดงหั่นเป็นสัน	1	เม็ด
น้ำมัน	¼	ถ้วย	แตงกวาหั่นเป็นแว่นหนา ¼ นิ้ว	6	ผล
หอมใหญ่หั่นตามขวาง ½ ซม.	100	กรัม	ต้นหอม	6	ต้น
ซอสมะเขือเทศ	2	ช้อนโต๊ะ	มะนาว	2	ผล

Rice Noodles with Chopped Beef

INGREDIENTS:

½ kg wide rice noodles
300 grams ground beef
2 tbsp. celery
2 tbsp. light soy sauce
½ tbsp. curry powder
2 tbsp. tapioca flour
2 tbsp. dark soy sauce
200 grams lettuce

1 tsp. chopped garlic
¼ cup cooking oil
1½ cup chicken stock
1 tbsp. sugar
1 pounded chilli pepper in 2 tbsp. vinegar
2 coriander or celery plants

PREPARATION:

- Separate the rice noodles, mix with ½ tbsp. dark soy sauce, and fry in 2 tbsp. oil. When well heated, remove from pan.
- Mix beef with light soy sauce, curry powder, and tapioca flour and allow to stand for a while.
- Wash and drain the lettuce, cut into short strips, and place in the bottoms of the serving plates. Arrange the noodles on the lettuce.
- Saute the garlic in remaining oil, add the beef mixture and fry until done, then add 1½ cups chicken stock, celery, and 1 tbsp. sugar. Spoon over the noodles, sprinkle with coriander or celery, and serve with chilli in vinegar.

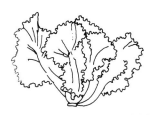

ก๋วยเตี๋ยวเนื้อสับ

เครื่องปรุง

ก๋วยเตี๋ยวเส้นใหญ่	$\frac{1}{2}$	กิโลกรัม	ผักกาดหอม	200	กรัม
เนื้อวัวบด	300	กรัม	กระเทียมสับ	1	ช้อนชา
ตังฉ่าย	2	ช้อนโต๊ะ	น้ำมัน	$\frac{1}{4}$	ถ้วย
ซีอิ๊วขาว	2	ช้อนโต๊ะ	น้ำซุป	$1\frac{1}{2}$	ถ้วย
ผงกระหรี่	$\frac{1}{2}$	ช้อนโต๊ะ	น้ำตาล	1	ช้อนโต๊ะ
แป้งมัน	2	ช้อนโต๊ะ	พริกแดงบด 1 เม็ดผสมกับน้ำส้ม	2	ช้อนโต๊ะ
ซีอิ๊วดำ	2	ช้อนโต๊ะ	ผักชีหรือต้นขึ้นฉ่าย	2	ต้น

Crispy Fried Noodles

INGREDIENTS:

150 grams thin rice noodles
¼ cup finely chopped fresh shrimp
¼ cup finely chopped pork
1 cake yellow soybean curd, cut to
    matchstick size pieces and fried crisp
1 tbsp. chopped garlic and shzllots
1 tbsp. fermented soybeans
1 tbsp. vinegar
1 tbsp. fish sauce

4 tbsp. palm sugar
1 tbsp lemon juice
1 tsp. ground dried chillies
50 grams bean sprouts
3 Chinese leek plants
1 chilli, finely sliced
1 coriander plant
2 pickled garlic bulbs, finely sliced
3 cups cooking oil

PREPARATION:

- If the noodles are very fine, fry in oil until crisp and golden, then drain. (If the noodles are thick, soak 15 minutes in water, drain well, and then fry a few at a time.)
- Heat ¼ cup oil in a frying pan. Fry garlic and shallots until fragrant, then add the pork and shrimp, seasoning with fermented soybeans, vinegar, fish sauce, sugar, and dried chillies.When thick, add the lemon juice, mix, taste, and season to obtain sweet, sour, and salty flavor.
- Reduce heat, add the noodles and continue turning them until they stick together, then add the bean curd and dip onto plates.
- Sprinkle with the pickled garlic, finely sliced lemon rind, coriander, and chilli and place bean sprouts and Chinese leek on the sides of the plates.

ผัดหมี่กรอบ

เครื่องปรุง

เส้นหมี่	150 กรัม	น้ำตาลปีบ	4	ช้อนโต๊ะ
กุ้งสดหั่นชิ้นเล็ก ๆ	¼ ถ้วย	น้ำมะนาว หรือน้ำส้มซ่า	1	ช้อนโต๊ะ
เนื้อหมูหั่นชิ้นเล็ก ๆ	¼ ถ้วย	พริกป่น	1	ช้อนชา
เต้าหู้เหลืองหั่นเล็ก ๆ เท่าก้าน		ถั่วงอก	50	กรัม
ไม้ขีดทอดกรอบ	1 แผ่น	กุยช่าย	3	ต้น
กระเทียมและหอมสับ	1 ช้อนโต๊ะ	พริกแดงหั่นฝอย	1	เม็ด
เต้าเจี้ยว	1 ช้อนโต๊ะ	ผักชี	1	ต้น
น้ำส้ม	1 ช้อนโต๊ะ	กระเทียมดองหั่นบาง ๆ	2	หัว
น้ำปลา	1 ช้อนโต๊ะ	น้ำมันสำหรับทอด	3	ถ้วย

Phad Thai Sai Khai : ก๋วยเตี๋ยวผัดไทยใส่ไข่

Phad Thai Sai Khai *(Fried Noodles Thai Style)*

INGREDIENTS:

300 grams narrow rice noodles
½ kg bean sprouts
3 eggs
50 grams pork, cut into small slivers
50 grams chopped pickled white radish
1 cake soybean curd, cut into small
  slivers
½ cup ground roasted peanuts
1 tsp. ground dried chillies
1 tbsp. chopped shallots

1 tbsp. chopped garlic
½ cup cooking oil
4 tbsp. sugar
3 tbsp. fish sauce
4 tbsp. tamarind juice or vinegar
50 grams Chinese leek leaves
1 lemon
1 banana flower
Indian pennywort leaves

PREPARATION:

● Heat 3 tbsp. oil in a frying pan and saute garlic and shallots. When yellowed, add noodles with just enough water to soften them and fry, turning constantly with spatula to prevent sticking. Then move noodles to side of pan or remove from pan.

● Put 3 tbsp. oil into pan. When hot, fry the pork, pickled white radish, bean curd, and dried chillies and then return the ·noodles, mix thoroughly, and move to side or remove.

● Put 2 tbsp. oil into the pan. When heated, break eggs into pan and scramble with spatula, spreading egg in a thin layer over the pan. When set, return the noodles and mix together. Add half the bean sprouts and the Chinese leek leaves and turn to mix together. Spoon onto plates and sprinkle with ground peanut. Serve with bean sprouts, banana flower, Chinese leek , and Indian pennywort.

Fried noodles require a lot of oil; however, it is possible to use less than indicated above by adding small amounts from time to time to keep the noodles from drying instead of adding all the oil at once.

ก๋วยเตี๋ยวผัดไทยใส่ไข่

เครื่องปรุง

ก๋วยเตี๋ยวเส้นเล็ก	300 กรัม	กระเทียมสับ	1	ช้อนโต๊ะ
ถั่วงอก	½ กิโลกรัม	น้ำมัน	½	ถ้วย
ไข่เป็ด	3 ฟอง	น้ำตาล	4	ช้อนโต๊ะ
เนื้อหมูหั่นเล็ก ๆ	50 กรัม	น้ำปลา	3	ช้อนโต๊ะ
หัวผักกาดเค็มสับ	50 กรัม	ส้มมะขามหรือน้ำส้ม	4	ช้อนโต๊ะ
เต้าหู้หั่นเล็ก ๆ	1 แผ่น	ใบกุยช่าย	50	กรัม
ถั่วลิสงป่น	½ ถ้วย	มะนาว	1	ผลใหญ่
พริกป่น	1 ช้อนชา	หัวปลี ใบบัวบก		
หอมสับ	1 ช้อนโต๊ะ			

Fried Sea Mussels

INGREDIENTS:

1 cup shelled sea mussels
1 cup tapioca flour
½ cup wheat flour
1½ cups water
6 eggs

½ kg bean sprouts
6 tbsp. fried garlic
pepper, spring onions cut into short
lengths, coriander leaves, fish sauce,
sugar, vinegar, and chillies

PREPARATION:

- Mix the tapioca and wheat flours with the water and divide the batter into six portions.
- Wash and drain the mussels and divide into six portions.
- Heat ¼ cup oil in a frying pan. When hot, place 1 tbsp. fried garlic in the oil.
- Place one portion of mussels in one portion of batter and pour onto the garlic in the pan. When batter solidifies, break an egg onto it and, with spatula, break and smear the egg over the surface of the batter. When batter is browned on the bottom, turn, break into pieces, and add about 1 tbsp. fish sauce or light soy sauce and about 1 tsp. sugar. Add about ½ cup washed bean sprouts, then dip onto plate and sprinkle with pepper and coriander leaves.
- Serve with sauce made by mixing 3 finely sliced chillies with 1 tbsp. sugar, 1 tsp. salt, and ½ cup vinegar.

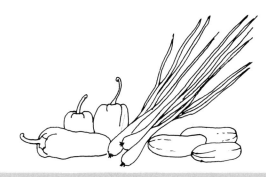

หอยแมลงภู่ทอด

เครื่องปรุง

หอยแมลงภู่แกะเปลือกออก			ถั่วงอก	$\frac{1}{2}$	กิโลกรัม
แล้ว	1	ถ้วย	กระเทียมเจียว	6	ช้อนโต๊ะ
แป้งมันเทศ หรือแป้งมัน	1	ถ้วย	พริกไทยป่น ต้นหอมตัดเป็นท่อน		
แป้งสาลี	$\frac{1}{2}$	ถ้วย	สั้น ผักชีเด็ดใบ น้ำปลา น้ำ		
น้ำ	$1\frac{1}{2}$	ถ้วย	ตาลทราย น้ำส้ม พริกชี้ฟ้า		
ไข่เป็ด	6	ฟอง	แดง		

Ba Mee Nong Kai : บะหมี่น่องไก่

Ba Mee Nong Kai *(Egg Noodles with Chicken Thigh)*

INGREDIENTS FOR EGG NOODLES:

2 cups wheat flour
1-2 egg yolks
1 tsp. salt
1 tbsp. cooking oil

¼ cup water in which Chinese mustard green was boiled, or ¼ cup plain water

PREPARATION OF NOODLES:

- Mix together the flour, salt, oil, and mustard green water and knead until dough is uniform, soft and sticky.
- Roll dough out thin, then roll up and cut into thin noodles with a sharp knife, using flour to prevent sticking. If a noodle cutter is available, after rolling, use the cutter to make the noodles, again using flour to prevent sticking. Then place the noodles in boiling water to which 1 tsp. salt has been added. When the noodles are done, dip up with strainer, drain, and mix with a little oil in which garlic has been fried.
- Blanch Chinese mustard green in boiling water, dip up, place in cold water for a moment, drain and cut into 1-2 inch lengths.

INGREDIENTS FOR CHICKEN IN SAUCE:

10 chicken thighs (about 1 kg)
1 tbsp. light soy sauce
2 tbsp. dark soy sauce
1 tbsp. Maggi sauce

2 tbsp. Mekhong whiskey or clear Chinese liquor
2 tsp. pepper
1 tsp. salt
1-2 tbsp. sugar

PREPARATION:

- Mix all ingredients in a pot and marinate the chicken thighs for 1 hour.
- Heat 4 cups oil in a frying pan and fry the chicken thighs over moderate heat until uniformly golden brown all over then remove from oil.
- Add 3 cups water to marinade, heat to boiling, and add ½ tbsp. each of Maggi sauce and dark and light soy sauces (more or less according to taste).
- Place some mustard green in each serving bowl, add noodles, a thigh, and some of the soup. Serve hot.

Barbequed Pork

INGREDIENTS:

1 kg pork shoulder cut into
    2 × 4 × 4 inch pieces
2 tbsp. light soy sauce
2 tbsp. sherry
1 tbsp. sesame oil

4 tbsp. sugar
1 tsp. salt
2 garlic plants cut into 1 inch lengths
2 tsp. juice from freshly pounded ginger
2 tbsp. honey

PREPARATION:

- Marinate pork in the other ingredients about six hours before barbecuing.
- While barbecuing, brush pork with marinade. When done, cut pork into small pieces and arrange on a platter. Serve with fresh vegetables and slices of cucumber and tomato.

หมูย่าง

เครื่องปรุง

เนื้อหมูตรงส่วนไหล่หั่นชิ้น			เกลือ	1	ช้อนชา
ขนาด 2×4×4 นิ้ว	1	กิโลกรัม	ต้นกระเทียมหั่นเป็นท่อนสั้น		
ซีอิ๊วขาว	2	ช้อนโต๊ะ	1 นิ้ว	2	ต้น
เหล้าเชอรี่	2	ช้อนโต๊ะ	ขิงสดตำคั้นเอาแต่น้ำ	2	ช้อนชา
น้ำมันงา	1	ช้อนโต๊ะ	น้ำผึ้ง	2	ช้อนโต๊ะ
น้ำตาล	4	ช้อนโต๊ะ			

บะหมี่น่องไก่

เส้นบะหมี่

แป้งสาลี	2	ถ้วย	น้ำมันพืช	1	ช้อนโต๊ะ
ไข่แดง	1–2	ฟอง	น้ำต้มผักกาดกวางตุ้ง	$\frac{1}{4}$	ถ้วย
เกลือป่น	1	ช้อนชา			

ส่วนผสมการปรุงน่องไก่

น่องไก่ประมาณ (1 กิโลกรัม)	10	น่อง	เหล้าแม่โขงหรือสุราขาวของจีน	2	ช้อนโต๊ะ
ซีอิ๊ว	1	ช้อนโต๊ะ	พริกไทยป่น	2	ช้อนชา
ซีอิ๊วดำ	2	ช้อนโต๊ะ	เกลือ	1	ช้อนชา
แม็กกี้	1	ช้อนโต๊ะ	น้ำตาลทราย	1–2	ช้อนโต๊ะ

Rice Noodles with Crab

INGREDIENTS:

2-3 crabs
1 cup crab meat
½ cup shallots
2 tbsp. garlic
5 dried chilli, seeds removed, soaked
   in water
¼ cup palm sugar

¼ cup tamarind juice
¼ cup fish sauce
300 grams bean sprouts
100 grams Chinese leek
¼ cup cooking oil
2-3 lemons
300 grams dried, narrow rice noodles
   (Chanthaburi noodles)

PREPARATION:

• Peel the garlic and shallots and slice the dried chilli. Place the chilli and the salt in a mortar and pound, then add the garlic and shallots and pound until ground and mixed thoroughly.
• Wash the crabs clean and cut each into 4-6 pieces, depending on size.
• Heat the oil in a frying pan. When hot, fry the pounded chilli paste and season to taste, then fry the crabs. When done, place in a pot.
• Soak the noodles in water about 5 miniutes, then drain.
• Divide the liquid remaining from the frying of the crabs into two portions.
• In one portion, fry the crab meat for sprinkling over the noodles.
• In the second portion, fry the noodles. Then add the bean sprouts, and the Chinese leek cut into short lengths, and the fried crabs and mix.
• Place noodles on plates and spoon fried crab meat over them. Serve with banana flower, Chinese leek, and lemon sections.

เส้นจันท์ผัดปู

เครื่องปรุง				
ปูม้าหรือปูทะเล	2-3	ตัว	น้ำส้มมะขาม	$\frac{1}{4}$ ถ้วย
เนื้อปูแกะแล้ว	1	ถ้วย	น้ำปลา	$\frac{1}{4}$ ถ้วย
หอมแดง	$\frac{1}{2}$	ถ้วย	ถั่วงอก	300 กรัม
กระเทียม	2	ช้อนโต๊ะ	ใบกุยช่าย	100 กรัม
พริกแห้งผ่าเอาเมล็ดออกแช่น้ำ	5	เม็ด	น้ำมัน	$\frac{1}{4}$ ถ้วย
น้ำตาลปีบ	$\frac{1}{4}$ ถ้วย		มะนาว	2-3 ผล
			เส้นจันท์	300 กรัม

Rume

INGREDIENTS:

1 cup ground pork
½ cup crushed roasted peanuts
½ cup ground fresh shrimp
¼ cup diced onion
¼ cup coriander leaves

2 thinly sliced chillies
3 tbsp. fish sauce
3 tbsp. sugar
1 tbsp. well pounded mixture of coriander root, pepper, and garlic
6 duck eggs, beaten

PREPARATION:

- Fry coriander root-pepper-garlic mixture until fragrant, add pork and fry until done, then add shrimp and onion and then fish sauce and sugar to taste. Add the peanuts and continue frying, mixing thoroughly, until dry, then remove from heat.
- Spread thin layer of oil over entire inner surface of a frying and place on low heat. When hot, dip hand into egg, then with fingers slightly spread, quickly move hand above surface of the pan, allowing thin streams of egg to fall onto the pan. Continue in this way crisscrossing the pan to make a net-like arrangement of fibers of egg. When egg is cooked, remove from pan.
- Place the egg net down so the smooth side is on the bottom. Make an X with sliced chilli in the center, then put on the coriander leaves, and finally the pork filling. Then fold up into a square as in the picture.
- An alternative way to make the egg net is to roll banana leaf into cones, fasten the cones closed, cut small openings in the points of the cones, and then attach two or three cones together. The cones are then filled with egg and moved back and forth, to and fro across the surface of the pan. This method is better than using the hand.

หรุ่ม

ส่วนผสม					
เนื้อหมูสับละเอียด	1	ถ้วย	พริกแดงหั่นฝอย	2	เม็ด
ถั่วลิสงบุบ	½	ถ้วย	น้ำปลา น้ำตาล อย่างละ	3	ช้อนโต๊ะ
กุ้งสดสับละเอียด	½	ถ้วย	รากผักชี พริกไทย กระเทียม	1	ช้อนโต๊ะ
หัวหอมใหญ่หั่นสี่เหลี่ยมเล็กๆ	¼	ถ้วย	โขลกละเอียด		
ผักชีเด็ดเป็นใบๆ	¼	ถ้วย	ไข่เป็ดตีพอเข้ากัน	6	ฟอง

Egg Rolls : ปอเปี๊ยะทอด

Egg Rolls *(Fried Poh Piah)*

INGREDIENTS:

25 grams mung bean noodles
100 grams chopped pork
1 egg
100 grams finely sliced cabbage
1 tbsp. chopped garlic
50 grams bean sprouts
1/4 tsp. pepper

1 tbsp. light soy sauce
300 grams small egg roll sheets (keep wrapped up to prevent drying out)
3 cups cooking oil
paste made by mixing 2 tbsp. wheat flour in 1/4 cup water and stirring over low heat

PREPARATION:

- Soak noodles until soft, then cut into short lengths. Blend pork, egg, cabbage, bean sprouts and light soy sauce together and then mix in the noodles.
- Fry the garlic in some oil and then add the pork and noodle mixture. Fry until fairly dry, then dip up and set aside to cool.
- Place a teaspoonful of filling on an egg roll sheet, fold the sheet over the filling, roll about half a turn, fold in the ends to close them, then roll up tightly, sealing the sheet closed with the paste. Fry in plenty of oil over low heat until crisp and golden brown. Serve with egg roll sauce, cucumber, and sweet basil leaves.

EGG ROLL SAUCE

1/4 cup vinegar
1/4 cup water
1/2 cup sugar
1 tsp. salt

1/2 chilli pepper, well pounded
2 tsp. tapioca flour mixed in 2 tbsp. water

.PREPARATION:

- Mix the vinegar, water, sugar, salt and chilli, heat to boiling, add a little of the flour water, boil a short time, then remove from heat.

ปอเปี้ยะทอด

ส่วนผสม

วุ้นเส้น	25	กรัม	พริกไทย	$\frac{1}{4}$	ช้อนชา
เนื้อหมูสับ	100	กรัม	ซีอิ๊วขาว	1	ช้อนโต๊ะ
ไข่	1	ฟอง	แป้งปอเปี้ยะแผ่นเล็ก	300	กรัม
กะหล่ำปลีหั่นฝอย	100	กรัม	น้ำมันสำหรับทอด	3	ถ้วย
กระเทียมสับ	1	ช้อนโต๊ะ	แป้งเปียก (แป้งสาลี 2 ช้อนโต๊ะ		
ถั่วงอก	50	กรัม	น้ำ $\frac{1}{4}$ ถ้วย กวนพอสุก		

น้ำจิ้ม

น้ำส้มและน้ำ	$\frac{1}{4}+\frac{1}{4}$	ถ้วย	พริกแดงโขลกละเอียด	$\frac{1}{2}$	เม็ด
น้ำตาลทราย	$\frac{1}{2}$	ถ้วย	แป้งมัน	2	ช้อนชา
เกลือ	1	ช้อนชา	น้ำละลายแป้งมัน	2	ช้อนโต๊ะ

Tapioca Balls with Pork Filling

INGREDIENTS:

1½ cup small tapioca pellets
1 cup finely chopped pork
½ - ¾ cup hot water
½ tsp. coriander root
¼ tsp. pepper
4 garlic cloves
3 tbsp. lard
3 tbsp. palm sugar

3 tbsp. fish sauce
1 cup chopped onion
½ cup ground peanuts
3 tbsp. fried garlic (for topping)
Fresh vegetables, such as lettuce
   and coriander
hot chillies

PREPARATION:

- Clean tapioca pellets. Adding hot water a little at a time, knead until soft and then let stand for a hour. Then form into ½ inch balls.
- Fry coriander root until fragrant. Add pork and fry until done, adding palm sugar and fish sauce to obtain sweet and salty taste. Add onion and continue frying until dry, then add peanuts, mix in, and dip out of pan.
- Flatten out tapioca ball into thin sheet, place 1-1½ tsp. filling on sheet and wrap up to form a secure ball. Line steamer tray with banana leaf, brush with cooking oil and place balls on leaf, taking care not to crowd balls in tray. Steam 15 minutes, remove from steamer, and sprinkle with fried garlic.
- Serve with fresh vegetables and hot chillies.

สาคูไส้หมู

เครื่องปรุง					
สาคูเม็ดเล็ก	$1\frac{1}{2}$	ถ้วย	น้ำปลา	3	ช้อนโต๊ะ
น้ำร้อน	$\frac{1}{2}-\frac{3}{4}$	ถ้วย	หอมใหญ่หั่นเล็ก ๆ	1	ถ้วย
รากผักชี	$\frac{1}{2}$	ช้อนชา	ถั่วลิสงป่น	$\frac{1}{2}$	ถ้วย
พริกไทย	$\frac{1}{4}$	ช้อนชา	กระเทียมเจียวสำหรับพรม	3	ช้อนโต๊ะ
กระเทียม	4	กลีบ	ผักสดผักกาดหอม ผักชี	200	กรัม
น้ำมันหมู	3	ช้อนโต๊ะ	พริกขี้หนู		
น้ำตาลปีบ	3	ช้อนโต๊ะ			

Yam Nua Yang : ยำเนื้อย่าง

Yam Nua Yang *(Barbecued Beef Salad)*

INGREDIENTS:

½ kg (2 cups) round, rump, or sirloin
  steak, grilled rare, sliced thin
2 onions, sliced thin
3-4 lettuce plants
coriander leaves
10 garlic cloves, crushed
20 hot chillies
5-6 cucumbers, sliced into rings

3 tbsp. fish sauce
3 tbsp. lemon juice
1 tbsp. sugar
thinly sliced chillies for garnishing
  (alternatively, chillies may be slit
  part of the way down the length
  from the tip, the skin being curled
  back to look like flowers).

PREPARATION:

- Mix garlic, hot chillies, fish sauce, lemon juice, and sugar, seasoning to obtain a spicy and toss with meat, noions, and cucumber, place on serving platter, and garnish with coriander and sliced chillies.
- The meat, onions, and cucumber may also be arranged separately on the platter with the chilli sauce in a bowl in the center. The meat, vegetables, and sauce are then mixed at table.

When garnished with hard boiled egg, this dish is called Yam Khamoi.

ยำเนื้อย่าง

เครื่องปรุง

เนื้อลูกมะพร้าวหรือสะโพก หรือ			พริกขี้หนู		โขลกรวม
สันใน ย่างพอสุก หั่นบาง ๆ				20	เม็ด
2 ถ้วย	½	กิโลกรัม	แตงกวา หั่นตามขวาง	5-6	ลูก
หอมใหญ่ ปอกล้างหั่นบาง ๆ	2	หัว	น้ำปลาดี	3	ช้อนโต๊ะ
ผักกาดหอม	3-4	ต้น	น้ำมะนาว	3	ช้อนโต๊ะ
ผักชีเด็ดเป็นใบ ๆ พอควร	1	ต้น	น้ำตาลทราย	1	ช้อนโต๊ะ
กระเทียม	10	กลีบ	พริกแดงหั่นฝอยสำหรับโรยหน้า		
			หรือจัก จัด		

Naem Sot

INGREDIENTS:

1 cup (200 grams) finely chopped pork
½ cup (100 grams) finely sliced boiled pig skin
2 tsp. salt
1 tbsp. sliced garlic
3-4 tbsp. lemon juice

½ cup finely sliced young ginger root
¼ cup sliced onions
¼ cup coriander and spring onions
½ cup roasted peanuts
2 lettuces
1-2 tbsp. hot chillies

PREPARATION:

- Mix salt with pork then fry over low heat until done, breaking the meat into small fragments. Remove from heat, allow to cool, and mix in pig skin thoroughly.
- Gently blend in garlic, lemon juice, ginger, and onion and season to taste.
- Spoon meat onto a bed of lettuce. Sprinkle with coriander and spring onion. Serve with peanuts, hot chillies, lettuces and other vegetables.

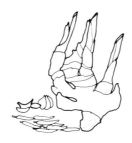

แหนมสด

เครื่องปรุง					
เนื้อหมูสับละเอียด	1	ถ้วย	ขิงอ่อนซอย	$\frac{1}{2}$	ถ้วย
	(200 กรัม)		หอมซอย	$\frac{1}{4}$	ถ้วย
หนังหมูต้มหั่นฝอย	$\frac{1}{2}$	ถ้วย	ผักชี ต้นหอมหั่นละเอียด	$\frac{1}{4}$	ถ้วย
	(100 กรัม)		ถั่วลิสงคั่ว	$\frac{1}{2}$	ถ้วย
เกลือ	2	ช้อนชา	ผักกาดหอม	2	ต้น
กระเทียมซอย	1	ช้อนโต๊ะ	พริกขี้หนู	1-2	ช้อนโต๊ะ
น้ำมะนาว	3-4	ช้อนโต๊ะ			

Coconut Rice Noodles

INGREDIENTS:

250 grams dried thin rice noodles
250 grams grated coconut
150 grams chicken or pork
100 grams yellow soy bean curd
300 grams bean sprouts
100 grams Chinese leek
1 egg
1-2 tbsp. cooking oil
6 finely chopped shallots

¼ cup fermented soy beans
2 tbsp. sugar
2 tbsp. tamarind juice
1-2 tsp. ground dried chillies
2 coriander plants, without roots
2 red chillies
2 lemons, sliced into wedges
banana flower
Indian pennywort leaves

PREPARATION:

- Soak the rice noodles in water 15 minutes to soften, then drain.
- Add 1 cup water to coconut, squeeze out 2 cups coconut milk, and heat until oil begins to come to surface, then remove and set aside.
- Slice the chicken or pork into small pieces.
- Cut bean curd into small,thin slices.
- Wash the bean sprouts and the Chiness leeks and cut into 1 inch lengths, saving the bases of the leeks to serve on the side.
- Heat 1 tbsp. oil in a frying pan, break egg into pan, scramble with spatula and spread thinly over bottom of pan. When firm, roll up and cut into long thin strips.
- Heat coconut milk in a frying pan and add shallots.When fragrant,add chicken or pork, fermented soy beans, sugar, bean curd, and dried chilli and cook together, seasoning to taste. Dip up about half the sauce to be used as a topping.
- Put the noodles in the remaining sauce and mix in well. Add the bean sprouts and Chinese leek leaf and mix in, then dip onto plates.
- Spoon sauce over the noodles and sprinkle with chopped coriander and chopped red chilli.
- Serve with bean sprouts lime wedges, Chinese leek, banana flower, and Indian pennywort.

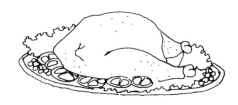

Lon Ham *(Coconut Ham Sauce)*

INGREDIENTS:

400 grams grated coconut

200 grams ham cut into small cubes
  (1 cup)

¼ cup minced shallots

½ cup fermented rice

6 chillies cut into short lengths

2-3 tbsp. tamarind juice

1 tbsp. palm sugar

2 tsp. salt

PREPARATION:

- Mix 1 cup water with the coconut and squeeze out 2 cups coconut milk.
- Place coconut milk in pot with the ham and fermented rice and heat to boiling. Add salt, tamarind juice, and palm sugar to taste, then add the shallots and chilli. When the sauce comes to a boil, remove from heat.
- Serve with fresh vegetables, such as cucumbers, cabbage, winged bean, string beans and lettuce.

หลนแฮม

เครื่องปรุง				
มะพร้าว	400	กรัม	พริกชี้ฟ้า เขียว เหลือง แดง	6	เม็ด
แฮมหั่นสี่เหลี่ยมเล็ก ๆ	200	กรัม		(ตัดท่อนสั้นๆ)
	(1 ถ้วย)		น้ำส้มมะขาม	2-3 ช้อนโต๊ะ
หอมซอย	$\frac{1}{4}$	ถ้วย	น้ำตาลปีบ	1	ช้อนโต๊ะ
ข้าวหมาก	$\frac{1}{2}$	ถ้วย	เกลือ	2	ช้อนชา

หมี่กะทิ

เครื่องปรุง					
เส้นหมี่	250	กรัม	น้ำมัน	1-2	ช้อนชา
มะพร้าว	250	กรัม	หอมเล็กสับละเอียด	6	หัว
เนื้อไก่หรือหมูหั่นชิ้นเล็ก ๆ	150	กรัม	เต้าเจี้ยว	$\frac{1}{4}$	ถ้วย
เต้าหู้เหลือง 1 แผ่นเล็ก หั่นชิ้น			น้ำตาลทราย	2	ช้อนโต๊ะ
เล็ก ๆ	100	กรัม	น้ำส้มมะขาม	2	ช้อนโต๊ะ
ถั่วงอก	300	กรัม	พริกป่น	1-2	ช้อนชา
กุยช่ายตัดท่อนสั้น ๆ 1 นิ้ว	100	กรัม	ผักชี	2	ต้น
(ส่วนโคนตัดยาว ๆ ไว้จัด			พริกแดง	2	เม็ด
จาน)			มะนาวผ่าเป็นชิ้น ๆ	2	ผล
ไข่เป็ด	1	ฟอง	หัวปลี ใบบัวบก		

Lon Tao Chiao *(Coconut Milk and Fermented Soy Bean Sauce)*

INGREDIENTS:

300 grams grated coconut
½ cup fermented soy beans
3 tbsp. chopped shrimp
3 tbsp. chopped pork
4 shallots
3-5 chillies

3 tbsp. sugar
3 tbsp. tamarind juice
salt (to be added only if desired as fermented soy beans are already very salty)

PREPARATION:

- Add ¾ cup water to the coconut and squeeze out 1½ cups coconut milk.
- Boil coconut milk in frying pan until oil comes to surface.
- Strain the fermented soy bean, place the solids in a mortar with 2 shallots and pound until mixed thoroughly. Dip up and mix with coconut milk in pan over low heat. Add the shrimp, pork, and chilli peppers and cook at low heat until done. Add 2 sliced shallots, and the palm sugar and tamarind juice to taste, bring to boil and remove from heat.
- Serve with fresh vegetables, such as cabbage, cucumbers, coriander, and young mango and hog plum leaves

หลนเต้าเจี้ยว

เครื่องปรุง					
มะพร้าว	300	กรัม	หอมซอย	4	หัว
ใส่น้ำ ¾ ถ้วย คั้นให้ได้	1½	ถ้วย	(หอมโขลกกับเต้าเจี้ยว 2 หัว)		
เต้าเจี้ยวขาว	½	ถ้วย	พริกชี้ฟ้า เหลือง แดง เขียว	3-5	เม็ด
เนื้อกุ้งสับ	3	ช้อนโต๊ะ	น้ำตาล	3	ช้อนโต๊ะ
เนื้อหมูสับ	3	ช้อนโต๊ะ	ส้มมะขาม	3	ช้อนโต๊ะ

Nam Phrik Kapi *(Shrimp Paste Chilli Sauce)*

INGREDIENTS:

2 tbsp. shrimp paste, roasted until fragrant

1 tbsp. chopped peeled garlic cloves

1 tbsp. ground dried shrimp

1 tsp. hot chilli, stems removed

1 tbsp. thinly sliced ripe ma-euk fruit

1 tbsp. thinly sliced rakam fruit (optional)

3 tbsp. lemon juice*

3 tbsp. fish sauce

2-3 tbsp. palm sugar

1 tbsp. thinly sliced makheua phuang or makheua pro fruits (eggplant)

When available, minced green mango, minced madan, or young tamarinds can be substituted for lemon juice.

PREPARATION:

- Place the garlic and shrimp paste in a mortar and pound until thoroughly mixed. Add dried shrimp and pound to mix in. Add hot chilli pepper, ma-euk, rakam, and makheua phuang and mix. Add sugar, fish sauce, and lemon juice to taste.
- Serve with vegetables, such as winged beans, string beans, bamboo shoots, gord gourd leaves, or water mimosa, boiled and topped with coconut cream;or with fresh vegetables, such as cucumbers, eggplant, swamp cabbage, cabbage or kathin; or with cha-om or long eggplant fried with egg.
- Accompanies fried mackerel, fried serpent head fish, or roasted catfish.

น้ำพริกกะปิ

เครื่องปรุง				
กะปิเผาไฟพอหอม	2	ช้อนโต๊ะ	ระกำซอย (ไม่ใส่ก็ได้)	1 ช้อนโต๊ะ
กระเทียมปอกเปลือกแล้วซอย			น้ำมะนาว	3 ช้อนโต๊ะ
หยาบ ๆ	1	ช้อนโต๊ะ	น้ำปลา	3 ช้อนโต๊ะ
กุ้งแห้งป่น	1	ช้อนโต๊ะ	น้ำตาลปีบ	2-3 ช้อนโต๊ะ
พริกขี้หนูเด็ดก้าน	1	ช้อนชา	มะเขือพวงบุบหรือมะเขือเปราะ	
มะอึกสุกหั่นฝอย	1	ช้อนโต๊ะ	ซอย	1 ช้อนโต๊ะ

Nam Phrik Long Rua Moo Wan : น้ำพริกลงเรือและหมูหวาน

Nam Phrik Long Rua Lae Moo Wan *(Sweet Pork with Hot Pepper Sauce)*

INGREDIENTS:

20 grams peeled garlic cloves
3 tbsp. shrimp paste
5 shredded madan fruits (or 1 green mango)
5 thinly sliced rakam fruits
5 thinly sliced ma-euk fruits (a kind of eggpant)
2 tbsp. lemon juice

1-2 tbsp. thinly sliced hot or ordinary chillies
½ cup finely ground good quality dried shrimp
4-5 tbsp. palm sugar
1 tbsp. cooking oil
½ cup sweet pork
1 salted egg
½ cup crumbled crisp fried catfish

PREPARATION:

- Place the garlic and shrimp paste in a mortar and pound until thoroughly mixed. Add the madan and pound to mix in thoroughly. Add the rakam and ma-euk and pound to mix in. Add the chilli and just break with pestle. Add the sugar.
- Heat oil in a frying pan and fry the chilli paste. Add the sweet pork and the dried shrimp. Taste and adjust flavor so it is sweet, sour, and salty.
- Place chilli paste on a serving plate. Cut salted egg into small cubes and sprinkle on the chilli paste together with the crisp fried catfish. Serve with fresh vegetables, such as cucumbers, cabbage, string beans, hog plum leaves, and eggplant.

SWEET PORK

INGREDIENTS:

100 grams thinly sliced pork
2 tbsp. palm sugar
2 tbsp. fish sauce

2 tbsp. thinly sliced shallots
2 tbsp. cooking oil

PREPARATION:

- Heat oil in frying pan. Add sugar and stir until fragrant. Add fish sauce and slices pork and fry over low heat. Add sliced shallots and simmer until pork is cooked and dry.

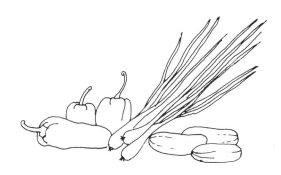

Nam Phrik Pla *(Fish Chilli Sauce)*

INGREDIENTS:

5-6 roasted fresh chillies
5 roasted shallots
2 roasted garlic bulbs
200 grams fish meat
1 tsp. fermented fish or shrimp paste

1 tbsp. salt
1½cups water
2 spring onion plants
2 coriander plants

PREPARATION:

- Remove skin from shallots and garlic, place in mortar with the chillies,and pound to mix together.
- Boil the water, add the fish and fermented fish,(or shrimp paste)and boil until done. Remove the fish meat, place in mortar, and pound to mix with chilli sauce. Strain the fish broth and mix about ¼ - ½ cup, or more if desired, with the chilli sauce. Place on serving dish with chopped spring onions and coriander.
- Serve with fresh or boiled vegetables.
  If preferred sour, add lemon juice or minced wild olive.

น้ำพริกปลา

เครื่องปรุง					
พริกสดเผา	5-6	เม็ด	ปลาร้า	1	ช้อนชา
หอมเผา	5	หัว	เกลือ	1	ช้อนโต๊ะ
กระเทียมเผา	2	หัว	น้ำ	1½	ถ้วย
เนื้อปลา	200	กรัม	ต้นหอม ผักชีหั่นหยาบ ๆ	2	ต้น

น้ำพริกลงเรือและหมูหวาน

เครื่องปรุง					
กระเทียมปอกเปลือกแล้ว	20	กรัม	กุ้งแห้งอย่างดีโขลกละเอียด	½	ถ้วย
กะปิ	3	ช้อนโต๊ะ	น้ำตาลปีบ	4-5	ช้อนโต๊ะ
มะดันซอย	5	ผล	น้ำมันสำหรับผัด	1	ช้อนโต๊ะ
ระกำหั่นบาง ๆ	5	ผล	หมูหวาน	½	ถ้วย
มะอึกหั่นบาง ๆ	5	ผล	ไข่เค็ม	1	ฟอง
น้ำมะนาว	2	ช้อนโต๊ะ	ปลาดุกฟูกรอบ	½	ถ้วย
พริกขี้หนู หรือพริกเหลืองหั่น					
บาง	1-2	ช้อนโต๊ะ			
เครื่องปรุง			น้ำปลาหรือซีอิ๊วขาว	2	ช้อนโต๊ะ
เนื้อหมูปนมันหั่นสี่เหลี่ยมเล็กๆ	100	กรัม	หอมซอย	2	ช้อนโต๊ะ
น้ำตาลปีบ	2	ช้อนโต๊ะ	น้ำมัน	2	ช้อนโต๊ะ

Khanom Jeen Sao Nam *(Vermicelli with Coconut Cream)*

INGREDIENTS:

1½ cups shredded fresh pineapple
¼ cup thinly sliced garlic
¼ shredded fresh ginger
½ cup ground dried shrimp
3 lemons
¼ cup fish sauce

¼ cup sugar
300 grams grated coconut
40 fish balls (see below)
1 kg vermicelli
15 hot chillies

PREPARATION:

• Add ¼ cup water to the coconut, squeeze out 1 cup coconut cream, and heat.
• Arrange vermicelli on plates, place fish balls, ginger, and garlic on top, and sprinkle with dried shrimp. Place pineapple and lemon slices on the side and pour hot coconut cream over the noodles. Serve with sugar and with sliced hot chilli peppers in fish sauce.

FISH BALLS

INGREDIENTS:

300 grams scraped fish meat
1 tbsp. roasted chilli curry paste
1 tbsp. coarsely cut coriander

1 tsp. salt and 1 tbsp. water mixed together

PREPARATION:

• Mix the scraped fish meat and dried chilli paste and add a little of the salt water. Continue kneading until stiff and then mix in the coriander. Mold into elongated balls and then either skewer and roast or boil in coconut milk.

ขนมจีนซาวน้ำ

เครื่องซาวน้ำ

สับปะรดสับละเอียด 1½ ถ้วย กระเทียมหั่นบาง ๆ ¼ ถ้วย ขิงสดหั่นฝอย ¼ ถ้วย กุ้งแห้งป่น ½ ถ้วย มะนาว 3 ผล น้ำปลาดี ¼ ถ้วย น้ำตาลทราย ¼ ถ้วย หัวกะทิข้น ๆ ตั้งไฟแล้ว 1 ถ้วย แจงรอนหรือ ลูกชิ้นปลา 40 ลูก ขนมจีน 25 จับ พริกขี้หนู 15 เม็ด

เครื่องทำแจงรอน

เนื้อปลาขูด 300 กรัม น้ำพริกแกงคั่ว 1 ช้อนโต๊ะ ผักชีหั่นหยาบ ๆ 1 ช้อนโต๊ะ เกลือ 1 ช้อนชา ผสม น้ำ 1 ช้อนโต๊ะ หอม 7 หัว กระเทียม 2 หัว ข่า 2 ช้อนชา ตะไคร้ 2 ช้อนโต๊ะ กระชาย 1 ถ้วย พริก แห้ง 3 เม็ดใหญ่ เกลือ 1 ช้อนชา กะปิ 1 ช้อนชา ปลาเค็ม 1 ชิ้น น้ำ 1 ถ้วย

Khanom Jeen Nam Ya *(Vermicelli and Fish Sauce)*

INGREDIENTS:

7 shallots, cut up coarsely
2 garlic bulbs
2 tsp. sliced galangal
2 tbsp. sliced lemon grass
1 cup minced krachai
3 dried chillies, seeds removed

1 tsp. salt
1 tsp. shrimp paste
1 one-inch thick piece of salted fish, roasted
1 cup water

Place all the above in a pot and simmer over low heat until soft. Remove from heat, cool, place in mortar, and pound to a fine paste.

OTHER INGREDIENTS:

400 grams grated coconut
1 meaty fish (200 grams)
2-3 tbsp. fish sauce
2 hard boiled eggs, each peeled and cut into 5 sections
1 kg vermicelli
½ of a bitter gourd, cut into thin slices and boiled

100 grams string bean, cut into short lengths and boiled a short time
100 grams boiled swamp cabbage, cut into thin slices
100 grams boiled bean sprouts
1 small bunch sweet basil (maenglak)
1 chilli
ground dried chillies

PREPARATION:

- Add 2½ cups water to the grated coconut and squeeze out 5½ cups coconut milk. Skim off ½ cup coconut cream and set aside to add at the end.
- Wash and clean the fish, removing head and entrails, and boil until done in 1 cup water. Save the water in which the fish was boiled.
- Remove the meat from the fish, add to the chilli paste in the mortar, and pound to mix thoroughly. Dip paste into a pot, mix in coconut milk, and heat to boiling. Add the fish broth and fish sauce and simmer, stirring regularly to prevent sticking. When the sauce has thickened and its surface glistens bright red, add the coconut cream and remove from heat.
- Spoon the hot sauce over the rice vermicelli, vegetables, and egg arranged on plates just before serving.

ขนมจีน–น้ำยา

เครื่องปรุง

หอม 7 หัว กระเทียม 2 หัว ข่า 2 ช้อนชา ตะไคร้ 2 ช้อนโต๊ะ กระชาย 1 ถ้วย พริกแห้งแกะเมล็ดออก
3 เม็ดใหญ่ เกลือ 1 ช้อนชา กะปิ 1 ช้อนชา ปลาเค็ม 1 ชิ้น น้ำ 1 ถ้วย

เครื่องปรุงอื่น

มะพร้าว 400 กรัม ปลาเนื้อ ๆ 200 กรัม น้ำปลา 2-3 ช้อนโต๊ะ ไข่ต้ม 15 นาที 2 ฟอง ขนมจีน
25–30 จับ มะระ $\frac{1}{2}$ ลูก ถั่วฝักยาว 100 กรัม ผักบุ้งต้ม 100 กรัม ถั่วงอกลวก 100 กรัม ใบแมงลัก
1 กำเล็ก พริกแดง 2 เม็ด พริกป่น

Khao Mok Kai : ข้าวหมกไก่

Banana and Glutinous Rice Steamed in Banana leaf : ข้าวต้มมัด

Khao Mok Kai (Rice Cooked with Chicken)

INGREDIENTS FOR SPICE MIXTURE:

1 tsp. roasted coriander seeds	2 cloves
½ tsp. roasted cumin seeds	3 cardamoms
¼ tsp. powdered tumeric	2 tsp. curry powder
⅛ tsp. pepper	1 tbsp. crushed chillies
¼ tsp. powdered cinnamon	1 tbsp. salt

OTHER INGREDIENTS:

350 grams rice	1 tbsp. chopped garlic
2½ cups water	10 sliced shallots
1 tsp. salt	¼ cup butter
½ kg chicken thighs	¼ cup cooking oil
¼ cup milk with 1 tsp. vinegar added	3 potatoes
(sour milk)	3 tbsp. saffron water (¼ tsp. saffron
1 tbsp. finely chopped fresh ginger	in water)

PREPARATION:

- Place spice mixture ingredients in a mortar and pound until ground and mixed thoroughly.
- Wash the rice, add water and salt, and cook without pouring off water. When half done, remove from heat.
- Heat some of the oil in frying pan and brown the sliced shallots.
- Cut chicken into 2 inch pieces. Marinate 1 hour in sour milk, chopped ginger and garlic, then fry until golden brown in oil used for browning shallots.
- Peel potatoes, cut lengthwise into long pieces about ½ inch across, and fry.
- Fry the rice in the remaining oil and then dip into a pot. Arrange fried chicken and potato on the rice and sprinkle with saffron water and fried shallots. Cover pot and cook over low heat until rice is done.
- Serve with cucumbers, pickled ginger, and a sauce made by dissolving ½ tsp. salt and 2 tbsp. sugar in ¼ cup vinegar.

ข้าวหมกไก่

เครื่องปรุง

ข้าวสาร 350 กรัม น้ำ 2$\frac{1}{2}$ ถ้วย เกลือป่น 1 ช้อนชา ไก่ตะโพก $\frac{1}{2}$ กิโลกรัม นมเปรี้ยว $\frac{1}{4}$ ถ้วย (นม $\frac{1}{4}$ ถ้วย ใส่น้ำส้มสายชู 1 ช้อนชา)ขิงสด 1 ช้อนโต๊ะ กระเทียมสับ 1 ช้อนโต๊ะ หอมซอย 10 หัว เนย $\frac{1}{4}$ ถ้วย น้ำมัน $\frac{1}{4}$ ถ้วย มันฝรั่ง 3 หัว หญ้าฝรั่งประมาณ $\frac{1}{4}$ ช้อนชา

น้ำจิ้ม พริกแดงบด 1 ช้อนโต๊ะ เกลือ $\frac{1}{2}$ ช้อนชา น้ำส้ม $\frac{1}{4}$ ถ้วย น้ำตาล 2 ช้อนโต๊ะ

น้ำพริกสำหรับผสมข้าวหมกไก่

ลูกผักชีคั่ว 1 ช้อนชา ยี่หร่าคั่ว $\frac{1}{2}$ ช้อนชา ขมิ้นผง $\frac{1}{4}$ ช้อนชา พริกไทย $\frac{1}{8}$ ช้อนชา อบเชยตีป่น $\frac{1}{4}$ ช้อนชา กานพลูตีป่น 2 ดอก ลูกกระวานตีป่น 3 ลูก ผงกะหรี่ 2 ช้อนชา พริกแดงบด 1 ช้อนโต๊ะ เกลือป่น 1 ช้อนโต๊ะ

Banana and Glutinous Rice Steamed in Banana Leaf *(Khao Tom Mat)*

INGREDIENTS:

½ kg glutinous rice (soaked or un-
  soaked)
400 grams grated coconut
½ cup sugar

2 tbsp. salt
10 bananas (Nam Wa variety)
1 cup black beans, boiled until soft
½ kg banana leaf

PREPARATION:

- Wash and drain the rice.
- Mix 1 cup water with the coconut and squeeze out 2 cups coconut milk.
- Dissolve the sugar and salt in the coconut milk and strain into a brass pan add the rice, then cook over low heat with constant stirring until mixture is dry.
- Peel the bananas and slice in half lengthwise.
- Tear the banana leaf from edge to midrib into pieces 7-8 inches wide and place together in pairs so the midrib side of one is opposite that of the other. Put some rice on the leaf, place a banana half on the rice, cover the banana with more rice, press several black beans into the rice, then wrap up in the leaf. If desired, tie the packet, then steam for 40-45 minutes.

If the rice has not been soaked, the packets must be tied securely and boiled for 1 hour.

ข้าวต้มมัด

ส่วนผสม					
ข้าวเหนียว	$\frac{1}{2}$	กิโลกรัม	เกลือป่น	2	ช้อนโต๊ะ
(จะแช่น้ำหรือไม่แช่ก็ได้)			กล้วยน้ำว้า	10	ลูก
มะพร้าว	400	กรัม	ถั่วดำต้มสุกนุ่ม	1	ถ้วย
น้ำตาลทราย	$\frac{1}{2}$	ถ้วย	ใบตอง	$\frac{1}{2}$	กิโลกรัม

Thong Ek : ทองเอก

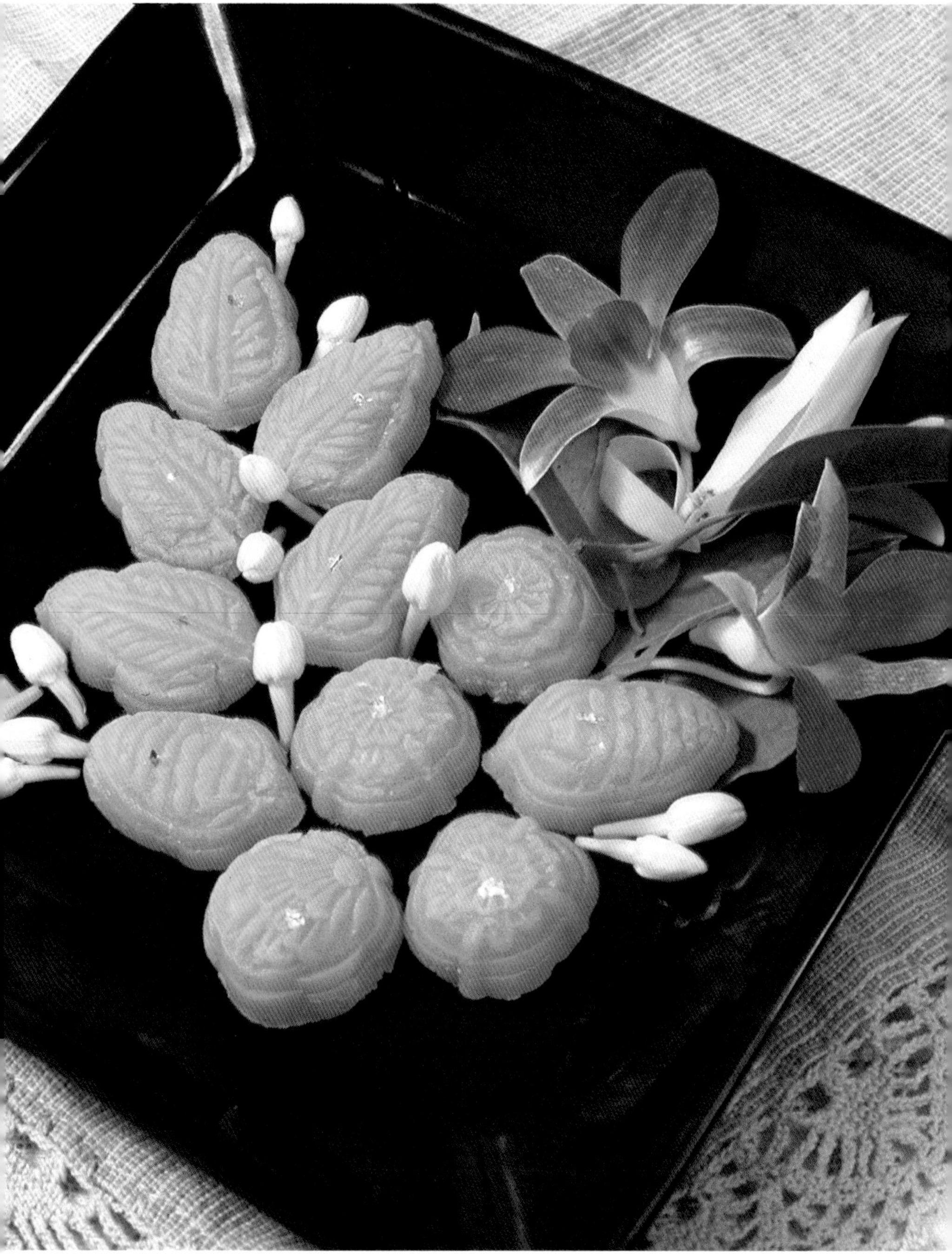

Thong Ek

INGREDIENTS:

1 cup sifted wheat flour

400 grams grated coconut

1 cup sugar

5-6 egg yolks

PREPARATION:

• Mix ¼ cup water with coconut, then squeeze out 1 cup coconut milk. Mix coconut milk with sugar, heat to boiling, remove from heat and strain.

• Heat sweetened coconut milk, simmering until thick (about the consistency of condensed milk), remove from heat, stir to cool, add the egg yolks one at a time.

• Heat batter a third time.When hot, add the flour slowly a little at a time. Cook about 5 minutes. When batter no longer sticks to pan, remove.

• While still warm, press molds down on batter. Use wooden molds. Knock to remove from mold. Store in tightly closed jar scented with jasmine and kradang-nga flowers.

ทองเอก

ส่วนผสม

แป้งสาลี	1	ถ้วย	น้ำตาลทราย	1	ถ้วย
มะพร้าว 4 ขีด คั้นกระทิ (ใส่น้ำ ¼ ถ้วย)	1	ถ้วย	ไข่แดง	5-6	ฟอง

Thong Yot *(Golden Drops)*

INGREDIENTS:

20 eggs

5 cups sugar

5 cups jasmine scented water

1 cup rice flour

PREPARATION:

- Mix the sugar and the water, heat to dissolve, strain, return to heat until boiling. Remove 1 cup of the sugar water to be used for soaking the thong yot.
- Return remaining sugar water to heat. When it begins to thicken, remove from heat.
- Break the eggs, separate yolks from whites, carefully remove all membrane from yolks, then beat until a lot of froth has formed. Take 1 cup of egg and mix with ¾ cup flour in a separate bowl and beat vigorously.
- Heat syrup to a strong boil. With thumb, index and middle fingers, grasp some batter, lift with sweeping motion across rim of bowl, then release smartly into the boiling syrup, continuing until pan is filled with thong yot. When done, remove with large spoon and transfer to sugar water.

ทองหยอด

ส่วนผสม

ไข่เป็ด	20	ฟอง	แป้งทองหยอดประมาณ	1	ถ้วย
น้ำตาลทราย	5	ถ้วย	(คือแป้งข้าวเจ้า)		
น้ำลอยดอกมะลิ	5	ถ้วย			

Thong Yip : ทองหยิบ

Thong Yip *(Golden Flower)*

INGREDIENTS:

20 eggs   5 cups jasmine scented water
5 cups sugar

PREPARATION:

- Mix sugar and jasmine water and then boil to the consistency of a syrup.
- Break eggs, separate yolks from whites, carefully remove all membrane from the yolks, beat the yolks until some froth forms, then allow to rest a while.
- Remove syrup from heat. Dip up some egg with a large spoon and drop enough into the hot syrup to form a lens 1½ inches in diameter. Repeat until the pan can accomodate no more such lenses, then return to heat. When done, remove from syrup and place on a tray or plate. While still warm, pinch around the top of each piece with thumb and forefinger to make 3-8 folds and then set into a small porcelain sweet cup. When the thong yip is cool and firm, remove from cup.

ทองหยิบ

ส่วนผสม
ไข่เป็ด   20   ฟอง   น้ำดอกไม้สด   5   ถ้วย
น้ำตาลทราย   5   ถ้วย

Foi Thong

INGREDIENTS:

10 duck eggs or eggs
5 hen's eggs

3 cups sugar
3 cups jasmine scented water

PREPARATION:

- Clarify sugar by breaking up egg shell in the sugar, mixing with jasmine water, heating until the sugar dissolves, and then straining. Continue heating to the consistency of syrup.
- Break eggs and separate yolks from whites. Collect the densest portion of the egg whites and set aside separately. Remove all membrane from the yolks and mix the yolks with 2-3 tbsp. of the dense portion of the whites.
- Heat syrup in copper pan over fairly low heat. Place egg in narrow stemmed funnel and moving the funnel in circles above the hot syrup, drop a thread of egg into the syrup, making 10-30 revolutions. When the egg has firmed (about 2 minutes), fold the thread over upon itself to form a raft, using a pointed wooden skewer. Then remove, and place in a jar scented with a fragrant candle and jasmine and kradang-nga flowers.

ฝอยทอง

ส่วนผสม					
ไข่เป็ด	10	ฟอง	น้ำตาลทราย	3	ถ้วย
ไข่ไก่	5	ฟอง	น้ำลอยดอกมะลิ	3	ถ้วย
ไข่น้ำค้าง	2-3	ช้อนโต๊ะ			

Custard Steamed in Pumpkin

INGREDIENTS:

1½ cups egg

¾ cup palm sugar

3 pandanus leaves

400 grams grated coconut

2 small pumpkins

PREPARATION:

- With a small, sharp pointed knife cut 5-6 pointed star-shaped opening around the stems of the pumpkins. Lift the stems and remove seeds and membrane from the insides.
- Mix ¼ cup warm water to coconut, then squeeze out 1½ cups coconut milk.
- Mix sugar with egg, beat with pandanus leaves for about 10 minutes, then continue beating, adding the coconut milk. Strain through cheesecloth into the pumpkins, filling them to within about 1 inch from the top.
- Support the base of each pumpkin in a bowl of the same size, place in steamer tray, putting the pumpkin stems beside the bowls in the tray, and steam over vigorously boiling water until cooked (about 45 minutes).

สังขยาฟักทอง

ส่วนผสม

ไข่เป็ด หรือไข่ไก่	1½	ถ้วย	มะพร้าว	400 กรัม
น้ำตาลปีบ	¾	ถ้วย	ใบเตย	3 ใบ

Pumpkin Pudding

INGREDIENTS:

450 grams peeled raw pumpkin (enough for 2 cups after steaming)

½ kg white grated coconut (reserve 50 grams for the pudding and another 50 grams for topping)

1 cup rice flour

¼ cup tapioca flour

½ tsp. salt

1 cup sugar

PREPARATION:

- Cut pumpkin into long 1 inch thick slices, steam until soft, then mash thoroughly.
- Add ¼ cup warm water to the remaining 400 grams of coconut and squeeze out 1¼ cups coconut milk.
- Blend pumpkin with rice and tapioca flours thoroughly, then add the sugar, 50 grams grated coconut, and ¼ tsp. salt and mix, adding the coconut milk a little at a time. Continue stirring until sugar has dissolved.
- Pour mixture into 8 × 8 inch baking pan and sprinkle with 50 grams grated coconut mixed with ¼ tsp. salt. When the water in the steamer is boiling, put the pan in the steamer tray and steam for 30 minutes. Then open the steamer, remove the pan, allow to cool, and cut the pudding into pieces of the desired size.

ขนมฟักทอง

ส่วนผสม				
ฟักทองดิบปอกเปลือกแล้ว (นึ่งสุกแล้วจะได้ 2 ถ้วย)	450	กรัม	แป้งข้าวเจ้า	1	ถ้วย
มะพร้าวขูดขาว (แบ่งออกไว้ใส่ในตัวขนม 50 กรัม โรยหน้า 50 กรัม)	$\frac{1}{2}$	กิโลกรัม	แป้งมัน	$\frac{1}{4}$	ถ้วย
			เกลือ	$\frac{1}{2}$	ช้อนชา
			น้ำตาลทราย	1	ถ้วย

Glutinous Rice Steeped in Coconut Milk

(Khao Niao Mun)

INGREDIENTS:

½ kg high quality glutinous rice
1 tbsp. salt
¾ cup sugar

½ kg white grated coconut or coconut cream ¾ cup, coconut milk 2¼ cup

PREPARATION:

- Clean the rice, picking out any grains of non-glutinous rice that may be mixed in, then soak the rice overnight, or at least 3 hours. Drain the rice, place in a steamer tray lined with cheesecloth, and steam until done (about 25-30 minutes after the water has begun to boil).
- Mix 1 cup warm water with coconut and squeeze out 2¼ cups coconut milk.
- Dissolve salt and sugar in the coconut milk, strain, and heat, stirring to prevent lumps. When coconut milk boils, remove from heat and set ¾ cup aside to be used when serving.
- When rice is done, place it in a container with a tightly fitting lid, pour in remaining coconut milk, stir vigorously, cover, and set aside for a while to allow the coconut milk to mingle with the rice thoroughly. When serving, spoon some of the coconut milk set aside earlier over the rice before adding toppings, such as, shrimp topping, custard, dried fish topping, or ripe mango.

When the rice is done, the coconut milk must be mixed in right away; otherwise, it will not be absorbed by the rice.

SHRIMP TOPPING

INGREDIENTS:

1 cup finely chopped shrimp
1 cup grated coconut (100 grams)
1 tsp. finely chopped coriander root
1 tsp. pepper

3 tbsp. cooking oil
2-3 tsp. salt
3 tbsp. sugar
2 tbsp. finely chopped kaffir lime leaves

PREPARATION:

- Chop shrimp and coconut together and add a little yellow coloring.
- Pound pepper and coriander root in mortar until ground and mixed thoroughly, fry in the oil until fragrant, then add shrimp and coconut and fry until done, seasoning to taste with salt and sugar. Remove from pan and sprinkle with chopped coriander.

CUSTARD

INGREDIENTS:

250 grams grated coconut
250 grams palm sugar

4 eggs

PREPARATION:
- Mix ½ cup water with coconut and squeeze out 1 cup coconut milk.
- Mix coconut milk, sugar, and eggs, beat with banana or pandanus leaf, strain into pan, and steam over vigorously boiling water for 25-30 minutes.

DRIED FISH TOPPING

INGREDIENTS:

1 dried serpent head fish (300 grams)	3 tbsp. sugar
2 tbsp. cooking oil	5 shallots, sliced thin and fried crisp
	salt

PREPARATION:
- Steam the fish until done, discard skin and remove meat from bones.
- Fry the fish meat in the oil over low heat until crisp, then add sugar and salt to obtain a sweet and salty taste. Remove from pan and sprinkle with fried shallots.

CANDIED COCONUT TOPPING (KRACHEEK)

INGREDIENTS:

2 cups shredded coconut	1½ cups water scented with jasmine
1½ cup palm sugar	

PREPARATION:
- Mix palm sugar with the water, heat until dissolved, add coconut and cook over low heat to a thick, syrupy consistency. Cool, then place in a lidded container scented with a fragrant candle.

ข้าวเหนียวมูล
ส่วนผสม
ข้าวเหนียวเม็ดงาม ๆ $\frac{1}{2}$ กิโลกรัม มะพร้าว $\frac{1}{2}$ กิโลกรัม เกลือป่น 1 ช้อนโต๊ะ น้ำตาลทราย $\frac{3}{4}$ ถ้วย

ข้าวเหนียวหน้ากุ้ง
ส่วนผสม
กุ้งสับละเอียด 1 ถ้วย มะพร้าวขูด (100 กรัม) 1 ถ้วย รากผักชีหั่น 1 ช้อนชา พริกไทยป่น 1 ช้อนชา
น้ำมัน 3 ช้อนโต๊ะ เกลือป่น 2–3 ช้อนชา น้ำตาลทราย 3 ช้อนโต๊ะ ใบมะกรูดหั่นฝอย 2 ช้อนโต๊ะ

ข้าวเหนียวหน้าสังขยา
ส่วนผสม
มะพร้าว 250 กรัม น้ำตาลปีบ 250 กรัม ไข่เป็ด 4 ฟอง

ข้าวเหนียวหน้าปลาแห้ง
ส่วนผสม
ปลาช่อนแห้งขนาด 300 กรัม 1 ตัว น้ำมัน 2 ช้อนโต๊ะ น้ำตาลทราย 3 ช้อนโต๊ะ หอมเล็กเจียวกรอบ
5 หัว เกลือป่น

ข้าวเหนียวหน้ากระฉีก
ส่วนผสม
มะพร้าวทึนทึกขูดกระต่ายจีน 2 ถ้วย น้ำตาลปีบ $1\frac{1}{2}$ ถ้วย น้ำลอยดอกมะลิ $1\frac{1}{2}$ ถ้วย

Khanom Thua Paep *(Mock Bean Pods with Shrimp Filling and*

with Sweet Filling)

PREPARATION OF DOUGH:

• Sift 3 cups glutinous rice flour into mixing bowl and add, a little at a time, 1 cup boiling water, stirring with wooden paddle. When the dough can be worked with the hands, knead until soft and uniform, then form into balls about ¾ inch in diameter, place on tray, cover with damp cloth, and set aside.

INGREDIENTS FOR SWEET FILLING:

1 cup mung beans, skins removed and steamed	¾ tsp. salt
	½ cup roasted sesame seeds
2 tbsp. grated white coconut	½ cup fine granulated sugar
	2 cups white shredded coconut

PREPARATION:

• Mix mung beans, 2 tbsp. grated coconut, and ¼ tsp. salt together. This is for filling the pods.

• Break sesame seeds open in mortar, then mix with the sugar and ½ tsp. salt. This is for sprinkling on the pods.

• Steam shredded coconut for 5 minutes. This is used for coating the pods.

INGREDIENTS FOR SHRIMP FILLING:

½ cup finely chopped shrimp	1 tsp. salt
½ cup finely chopped grated coconut	1 tsp. sugar
1 tbsp. well pounded mixture of coriander root, pepper, and garlic	1 tbsp. palm sugar
	2 finely sliced kaffir lime leaves
1 tbsp. cooking oil	300 grams grated coconut (for coconut milk)

PREPARATION:

• Fry the coriander root-pepper-garlic mixture in the oil until fragrant, then add the shrimp and finely chopped coconut and mix well. If cakes form remove pan from heat and break them up, then continue cooking. Add salt and sugar to taste. (There should be a sweet taste.) Then remove the shrimp filling from pan and sprinkle with kaffir lime leaf.

• Mix grated coconut with ¼ cup water, then squeeze out 1 cup coconut milk. Bring coconut milk to a boil, then remove from heat. This is poured onto the pods.

FILLING THE PODS:

• Press the dough balls out into discs ¼ inch thick. Place about a teaspoonfull of whichever filling in the center, fold over, and pinch securely closed along the edge. (Shape look like a bean pod.)

• Fill a large pan with water and bring to a boil. Drop pods into the water, boil until they float to surface (about 2-3 minutes), then dip up from the water.

- Upon removal, pods with sweet filling are shaken to remove excess water, immediately tossed with the steamed shredded coconut to coat them completely, then placed on a dish and sprinkled with the sesame and sugar mixture.
- Pods with shrimp filling are drained, placed on dish, topped with coconut milk and served with coriander.

ขนมถั่วแปบไส้เค็ม/หวาน

ส่วนผสม

แป้งข้าวเหนียว	3	ถ้วย	น้ำเดือด	1	ถ้วย

ไส้หวาน

ถั่วเขียวเราะเปลือกนึ่งแล้ว	1	ถ้วย	เกลือ	$\frac{1}{2}$	ช้อนชา
ผสมให้เข้ากันสำหรับใส่ไส้			ผสมงากับน้ำตาล และเกลือรวม		
งาคั่วให้หอมบุบให้แตก	$\frac{1}{2}$	ถ้วย	กันสำหรับไว้โรยหน้า		
น้ำตาลทรายละเอียด	$\frac{1}{2}$	ถ้วย	มะพร้าวสำหรับคลุกนึ่งแล้ว	2	ถ้วย

ไส้กุ้ง

กุ้งสับ	$\frac{1}{2}$	ถ้วย	เกลือป่น	1	ช้อนชา
มะพร้าวขูดสับละเอียด		$\frac{1}{2}$	น้ำตาลทราย	1	ช้อนชา
รากผักชี พริกไทย กระเทียม	1	ช้อนชา	น้ำตาลปีบ	1	ช้อนโต๊ะ
โขลกแล้ว			ใบมะกรูดหั่นละเอียด	2	ใบ
น้ำมัน	1	ช้อนโต๊ะ	มะพร้าวสำหรับคั้นกะทิ	300	กรัม

Khanom Somanat : ขนมโสมนัส

Khanom Somanat

INGREDIENTS:

2¼ cup grated coconut, pan roasted
until golden
1½ cups fine granulated sugar

½ cup egg white
2 tbsp. cocoa
1 tbsp. lemon
oil for greasing pan

PREPARATION:

- Beat egg whites fluffy, then continue beating, adding the sugar a little at a time until all has been incorporated, then beat in lemon juice.
- Blend in the roasted coconut and then the cocoa.
- Drop teaspoonsful of the mixture onto a greased baking pan. Bake at 350° F. until golden. Remove from oven and cool on rack. Store in a closed container.

ขนมโสมนัส

ส่วนผสม

มะพร้าวขูดแล้วคั่วให้เหลือง	$2\frac{1}{4}$	ถ้วย	โกโก้ผง	2	ช้อนโต๊ะ
น้ำตาลทรายป่นละเอียด	$1\frac{1}{2}$	ถ้วย	น้ำมะนาว	1	ช้อนโต๊ะ
ไข่ขาว	$\frac{1}{2}$	ถ้วย	น้ำมันสำหรับทาถาด		

Cotton Ball Cakes *(Khanom Pui Fai)*

INGREDIENTS:

2 duck eggs

1 cup palm sugar

1½ cups cake flour

1 tbsp. lemon juice

3 tbsp. water

2 drops jasmine water or 1 tsp. vanilla
extract

PREPARATION:

- Beat the eggs, adding the sugar a little at a time, until the mixture no longer drops from the beater when raised.
- Fold in the flour 2 tbsp. at a time, moving the spoon gently up from the bottom of the bowl to the top. When the first portion of flour is blended in, add a little of the water mixed with the lemon juice and the vanilla or jasmine water. Continue in this way alternating additions of flour and liquid until all the flour and liquid have been added. The last addition should be flour and all ingredients should be blended in well.
- Spoon the batter into paper cake cups held in small porcelain sweet cups. Fill each paper cup with batter. Arrange the porcelain cups in the steamer tray. Do not cover the holes in the steamer tray. The cups should be placed so steam rises all around them in order that the tops of the cakes have a pleasing appearance.
- Fill the bottom of the steamer three-quarters full of water and heat to a rolling boil, then reduce the heat to a slow boil, put the trays on the steamer, fit the lid tightly, and steam for about 15 minutes until the cakes are done.
Note: If all-purpose flour is used, add another tablespoon of water.

ขนมปุยฝ้าย

ส่วนผสม					
ไข่เป็ด	2	ฟอง	น้ำ	4	ช้อนโต๊ะ
น้ำตาลทราย	1	ถ้วย	กลิ่นมะลิ หรือวานิลลา (วานิลลา		
แป้งเค้ก	1½	ถ้วย	1 ช้อนชา หรือมะลิ 2 หยด)		
น้ำมะนาว	1	ช้อนโต๊ะ			

Crisp Pomegranate Seeds : ทับทิมกรอบ

Crisp Pomegranate Seeds *(Thabthim Grob)*

INGREDIENTS:

1 cup diced boiled water chestnuts (300 grams, or 40 fresh water chestnuts)

½ cup tapioca flour

150 grams sugar

¾ cup water (for syrup)

250 grams white grated coconut

ice

red food coloring

PREPARATION:

- Place red food coloring in a little water and soak the water chestnut until colored. Remove and place in the flour so the pieces become well coated. Then place these "pomegranate seeds" in a strainer to allow excess flour to fall away.
- Heat 5 cups water to boiling, boil the pomegranate seeds 3 minutes, remove, place in cold water, remove, and wrap in a thin white cloth.
- Mix ¼ cup water with the coconut and squeeze out ¾ cup coconut milk.
- Boil the sugar and the water to make syrup, allow to cool, then add the coconut milk.
- When serving, place the pomegranate seeds in dessert dishes and add syrup and ice.

ทับทิมกรอบ

ส่วนผสม

แห้วต้มหั่นสี่เหลี่ยมเล็ก ๆ	1	ถ้วย	น้ำทำน้ำเชื่อม	$\frac{3}{4}$	ถ้วย
(ถ้าแห้วดิบ 300 กรัมได้ 40 เม็ด)			มะพร้าวขาว	250	กรัม
แป้งมัน	$\frac{1}{2}$	ถ้วย	น้ำแข็ง		
น้ำตาลทราย	150	กรัม	สีขนมสีแดง		

Mango with Sweet Fish Sauce

INGREDIENTS:

½ kg palm sugar
¼ cup water
¼ cup fish sauce

½ cup chopped shallots
½ cup ground dried shrimp
2 finely sliced hot chillies

INGREDIENTS:

- In a pot large enough that it will be less than half full to prevent boiling over when additions are made, mix sugar, water, and fish sauce and simmer over low heat, stirring constantly. When the mixture has become a thick syrup, add the shallots. When shallots are done, remove from heat, blend in the dried shrimp, add the chillies, and stir.
- Peel about ten fully grown green mangos still slightly sour and cut into slices about ½ cm thick. If cut too thin, the slices will become limp quickly.
- Place in a container and chill in refrigerator to improve flavor and crispness.

มะม่วง–น้ำปลาหวาน

เครื่องปรุง					
น้ำตาลปีบ	$\frac{1}{2}$	กิโลกรัม	หอมซอย	$\frac{1}{2}$	ถ้วย
น้ำ	$\frac{1}{4}$	ถ้วย	กุ้งแห้งป่น	$\frac{1}{2}$	ถ้วย
น้ำปลา	$\frac{1}{4}$	ถ้วย	พริกขี้หนูหั่นบาง ๆ	2	เม็ด

Mango Juice : น้ำมะม่วง

Mango Juice

INGREDIENTS:

2 green Tawaai variety mangos or 2 ripe sour variety mangos

½-1 tsp. salt

½ cup syrup (½ cup sugar boiled in 1 cup water until thick)

1½ cups boiled water

PREPARATION:

- Peel, wash, and drain mangos, then cut into small slices. Place ½ cup of slices in an electric blender, add water, and blend. Add syrup and salt. The juice should have a pronounced sweet and sour taste to offset dilution when ice is added.

น้ำมะม่วง

ส่วนผสม

มะม่วงทะวายดิบหรือมะม่วง เปรี้ยวแก่จัด	2	ผล	
น้ำเชื่อม (น้ำตาล ½ ถ้วย กับน้ำ ½ ถ้วย ทำน้ำเชื่อม)	½	ถ้วย	
เกลือ			½-1 ช้อนชา
น้ำสุก			1½ ถ้วย

Jujube Juice

INGREDIENTS:

15 slabs candied jujube

10 cups water

1½ cups sugar

1 tsp. salt

PREPARATION:

- Wash jujube slabs quickly, place loosely in cheesecloth, and tie cloth closed securely.
- Heat water and place the bag in the water. Boil over reduced heat about 1½ hours.
- Remove bag from water, add sugar and salt, strain if necessary, and allow to cool. Serve with ice.

น้ำพุทรา

ส่วนผสม					
พุทราแผ่น	15	แผ่น	น้ำตาลทราย	$1\frac{1}{2}$	ถ้วย
น้ำ	10	ถ้วย	เกลือ	1	ช้อนชา

Star Gooseberry Juice : น้ำมะยม

Bael Fruit Juice : น้ำมะตูม

Pandanus Leaf Juice : น้ำใบเตย
Guava Juice : น้ำฝรั่ง

Star Gooseberry Juice

INGREDIENTS:

1 cup small slices of star gooseberry flesh

3 cups water

1 cup sugar

1 tsp. salt

PREPARATION:

- Boil star gooseberry slices in the water until soft. Place in electric blender and blend, then strain to remove star gooseberry flesh. Add sugar and salt to the juice, boil about half an hour over low heat, then remove from heat. Serve with ice.

ส่วนผสม	น้ำมะยม			
เนื้อมะยมหั่นชิ้นเล็ก ๆ	1	ถ้วย	น้ำตาล	1	ถ้วย
น้ำ	3	ถ้วย	เกลือ	1	ช้อนชา

Bael Fruit Juice

INGREDIENTS:

100 grams dried bael fruit slices

10 cups water

2 cups sugar

PREPARATION:

- Wash bael fruit slices and roast until fragrant.
- Bring water to a boil, add bael fruit slices and boil about 1½ hours over low heat.
- Remove bael fruit, add sugar, strain, and allow to cool. Serve with ice.

ส่วนผสม	น้ำมะตูม			
มะตูมแห้ง	100	กรัม	น้ำตาลทราย	2	ถ้วย
น้ำ	10	ถ้วย			

Pandanus Leaf Juice

INGREDIENTS:

1 cup dried pandanus leaf
5 cups water

1 cup sugar
1-2 cups ice

PREPARATION:

- In a pot with a tightly fitting lid, boil the water, add the pandanus leaf, stirring to submerge the leaf, cover, and boil for about 5 minutes. Strain to remove leaf, add sugar and stir to dissolve. Strain again and allow to cool. Serve with ice.

DRYING PANDANUS LEAVES

- Wash fresh pandanus leaves then cut into thin slices. Dry in the sun or in a low oven (200° F.), turning at intervals to ensure even drying. Store in a tightly lidded jar. Fresh leaves may also be used to make pandanus juice, following the recipe above.

น้ำใบเตย

ส่วนผสม				
ใบเตยหั่นฝอยตากแห้ง	1	ถ้วย	น้ำตาลทราย	1	ถ้วย
น้ำ	5	ถ้วย	น้ำแข็ง	1–2	ถ้วย

Guava Juice

INGREDIENTS:

2 cups small slices of fully ripe guava
6 cups water

½ cup sugar
1 tsp. salt

PREPARATION:

- Place guava slices in electric blender with water and blend thoroughly.
- Heat the juice and add sugar and salt. When juice comes to a boil, remove from heat. Can be served with ice.

น้ำฝรั่ง

ส่วนผสม				
ฝรั่งแก่จัดหั่นชิ้นเล็ก ๆ	2	ถ้วย	น้ำตาลทราย	$\frac{1}{2}$	ถ้วย
น้ำ	6	ถ้วย	เกลือ	1	ช้อนชา